Astonishing but True
Golf Facts

Astonishing but True
Golf Facts

———

Allan Zullo

———

**Andrews McMeel
Publishing**

Kansas City

02 03 04 05 BIN 10 9 8 7 6 5 4

Library of Congress Cataloging-in-Publication Data

Zullo, Allan.
    Astonishing but true golf facts / Allan Zullo.
        p.cm.
    ISBN 0-7407-1426-0 (pbk.)
    1. Golf-Miscellanea. I. Title.

GV967 .Z84 2001
796.352-dc21

00-053820

To Frankie Linquist, a young golfer destined for greatness—and that's a fact.

CONTENTS

Tee Time

The history of golf boasts a rich heritage of incredible incidents, hilarious happenings, fantastic feats, and remarkable records.

This book chronicles a sampling of the people, places, and events in golf that hopefully will astound, baffle, and amuse you. It's chock full of more than 500 intriguing facts like:

- The pro golfer whose wayward shot landed in the hot dog of a spectator.

- The amateur who nailed back-to-back holes in one—on consecutive par 4s.

- The British Open contender who needed 11 shots to get out of a bunker—and still won.

Astonishing but True Golf Facts

- The pro who took 12 strokes to hole out from only three feet.
- The Australian who walloped a drive more than one and a half miles.

From weekend matches to country club tourneys to the prestigious majors, golf will continue to amaze, confound, and delight us—just like this collection of fascinating facts hopes to do.

Amazing Shots
and Rounds

The second double eagle in Masters history was scored by a golfer who never even had the joy of watching the ball go into the cup. On the first day of the 1967 tournament, Australian Bruce Devlin was on the 530-yard, par-5 8th hole when he walloped a 290-yard drive. Unable to see the green from his position on the fairway, Devlin used a four-wood for his second shot. The ball hit in front of the green, took a big bounce, rolled toward the cup, hesitated on the front lip, and then dropped in as the crowd went wild. Thirty-two years earlier, Gene Sarazen scored the Master's first double eagle on the 15th hole.

Gene Sarazen said that his amazing double eagle 2 on the 15th hole at Augusta National in 1935 was not the greatest shot of his life. He made his best shot during a Ryder Cup match at Scioto Country Club in Columbus, Ohio, in 1931 against Fred Robson. Sarazen's tee shot went over the green and into a refreshment stand. "I found my ball in the middle of the stand in a crevice in the concrete," Sarazen recalled. "No free drops back then. A window toward the green was open, so I played the ball through the window and onto the green about eight feet from the hole." That, Sarazen said, was his greatest shot. "Robson three-putted and I sank my putt to win the hole."

Pro Richard Beckmann of Valdosta, Georgia, and amateur Frank Mulherin, of Augusta, Georgia, were locked in a two-man sudden death playoff for the last qualifying spot of the 1957 U.S. Open. On the 401-yard, par-4 1st hole, Mulherin struck a five-iron for his second shot and put the ball three feet away from the hole. "Match that," he crowed to his opponent. Beckmann did better than that. His five-iron shot ended up in the cup for an eagle 2 and a precious spot in the Open.

Actor Fred Astaire, a low-handicap golfer, proved his skill one day in 1938 while making the film *Carefree*. The script called for Astaire to strike a dozen golf balls with a driver in rhythm while he danced—all filmed as a continuous scene. Astaire was flawless, and after the scene, the crew went to retrieve the golf balls. To their astonishment, the staffers found all the balls within eight feet of one another.

Ken Venturi was taping some golf tips for a 1980 telecast, which included demonstrating a wedge shot. After hitting a few practice balls, Venturi told the cameraman to start shooting. "The wedge shot from 70 yards requires a lot of knee action and a smooth stroke," Venturi said into the camera. "And if this shot is hit correctly, the ball should take three bounces, jump left, and go into the hole." Venturi took a swing and, to his amazement, saw the ball take three bounces, jump to the left, and fall into the hole. The cameraman was so excited he shouted, "He sank the S.O.B.!"

At the 1984 Crosby at Pebble Beach, it looked as if Hale Irwin's chances of winning were on the rocks. Irwin hooked his drive terribly on the last hole of the tournament, but the ball hit a rock and bounced back into the fairway. He went on to par the hole and win a playoff.

Amazing Shots and Rounds

Among the historic plaques commemorating great golf shots around the world is the one at Westchester Country Club in New York in the middle of the 18th fairway. It marks the spot where Bob Gilder stood to hole his 230-yard three-wood second shot for a double eagle to win the 1982 Hanover Westchester Classic.

When Babe Didrikson Zaharias closed out Mrs. Don Chandler to win the Texas Women's Closed championship in 1935, Babe's winning stroke was a sand wedge out of wet mud in the left rough. She splashed the ball out, lost her balance, and fell into the muck. But her ball bounded onto the green—and into the hole for an eagle and the victory.

Astonishing but True Golf Facts

Gary Player is regarded as one of the best bunker players in the world. He proved that his reputation was well deserved in the 1990 British Open at Royal Birkdale in England. Player was in nine bunkers in all. Eight times he got up and down in two strokes. The ninth time he holed out.

In the 1985 Masters tournament, Bernhard Langer made one of the most remarkable shots in the event's history. In the third round, on the 13th hole, with its treacherous creek guarding the green, Langer had a bad lie among the trees. With 215 yards to carry the creek, he played a three-wood, but the ball landed short of the creek. Incredibly, the ball took a big bounce right over the water and stopped 18 feet from the hole. Langer made his two-under eagle 3 and went on to win the Masters by two shots.

Amazing Shots and Rounds

Nancy Lopez set an LPGA record when she shot four sub-70 rounds at the 1997 U.S. Women's Open. However, the sparkling scores of 69-68-69-69 weren't good enough to give Lopez her first Open win. England's Alison Nicholas used a record-setting performance of her own—a 10-under-par 274—to carve out a win by two strokes at Pumpkin Ridge Golf Club.

In 1997, four Englishmen played the longest day match in history when they completed 306 holes on the Akureyri Golf Club in northern Iceland, where it stayed light around the clock. To set the single-day record, tireless competitors Tom Hawkins, Tom Priday, Bruce Hopkins, and James Male divided up into two-man teams, using only two clubs each and playing one-ball in a format of alternating shots. Male and Hawkins won the match, 1,573 strokes to 1,614 strokes.

Astonishing but True Golf Facts

Four Aberdeen University students tried to golf their way up Scotland's 4,406-foot Mount Ben Nevis in 1961, but had to concede victory to the mountain. After losing 63 balls and using 659 strokes, they retired.

Talk about comebacks. George Duncan was 13 shots behind in the final round, yet still won the 1920 British Open. Seven years later at the Irish Open at Portmarnock, he was 14 shots behind in the last round, and came back to win the tournament.

The weirdest closing round in Masters history was shot in 1993 by winner Bernhard Langer, whose even-par 72 included only four pars. For the other 14 holes, Langer had seven birdies and seven bogeys.

In 1948, Murray "Moe" Norman, the eccentric Canadian pro, arrived at the last hole, needing a four to break the course record. He asked his playing partner what kind of hole it was. "Drive and nine-iron," Norman was told. So he hit his nine-iron off the tee and followed with a wood off the fairway. The ball came to rest within a foot of the flag. Norman scored a birdie 3—and broke the record.

Astonishing but True Golf Facts

At the 1968 U.S. Open, winner Lee Trevino tore up the Oak Hill course en route to becoming the first golfer ever to shoot all four rounds under par in the event. Trevino finished the tournament with a terrific total score of 275 and sizzling single rounds of 69-68-69-69.

The quickest recorded match at the Old Course in St. Andrews was played in 1922 by Jock Hutchison and Joe Kirkwood, who completed their competition in one hour and 20 minutes, when Hutchison closed out a 4-and-3 victory. That's compared with an average four hours per round played at that site.

It took more than ptomaine poisoning to keep "The Haig" down. The day before the 1914 U.S. Open, Walter Hagen suffered severe cramps from eating bad fish. The next day, he tied the course record at Midlothian Country Club in Blue Island, Illinois, with a 68 and went on to win the tournament by one shot over Chick Evans.

If equipment is lowering scores so drastically, how come English pro Alfred Edward Smith shot the lowest recorded 18-hole score on a regulation course more than a half century ago? Smith carded a 55 (15-under) on the Woolacombe course in 1936— a score that has yet to be beaten.

When Arnold Palmer went over to St. Andrews to play in the 1960 British Open, he shot a pitiful 47 on the first nine of his practice round with Roberto de Vicenzo and Max Faulkner. He finished the round with an embarrassing total of 86. But when it really counted, Arnie shook off his awful practice round in the tourney and fired a 279, placing him second to Kel Nagle, the winner.

The good news was that PGA Tour veteran Carl Cooper had belted the longest drive in tournament play at the 1992 H.E.B. Texas Open. The bad news was that he blasted his tee shot 331 yards *beyond* the par-4 green. Using an oversized driver on the 456-yard 3rd hole, Cooper pushed his tee shot way right. The ball landed on a cart path, bounced down a hill, and stopped an astounding 787 yards from the tee. Cooper needed three more shots just to reach the green, and he made a double-bogey 6 for his history-making mess.

Credit for the longest ball ever hit on earth goes to Australian weatherman Nils Lied. He teed one up at Mawson Base,

Antarctica, in 1962 and really crushed it. The ball traveled 2,640 yards from the makeshift tee, nearly one and a half miles. The prodigious clout was aided by wind and a landing area covered entirely in polar ice.

Once he cured himself of a terrible case of the hooks, Ben Hogan was renowned for his uncanny accuracy with the driver. But even Hogan outdid himself in the 1953 British Open at Carnoustie, Scotland. During the four rounds, his drives on the 18th hole were almost identical. In fact, his divots from his second shots on that hole were all located in a space of about one square yard.

When Doug Ford blasted from the left front bunker at the 72nd hole of the 1957 Masters, the ball went into the hole to give him the victory over Sam Snead. Ford exclaimed: "My God, that's the greatest shot of my life!"

Talk about well-matched opponents. In 1950 at Scotland's Bruntsfield Links club championship, W. S. Montford and Charles Greenock found the balls from their tee shots were touching in the middle of the fairway . . . on two different holes. The balls were resting together after the golfers' drives at the 363-yard 12th hole and then again on the 425-yard 15th hole. The match went five extra holes, with Greenock holing a chip to win.

Gary Player was regarded as the finest bunker player of his day, and he regularly astounded onlookers with his prowess with a sand wedge. One day in 1960 in a practice round near

Johannesburg, South Africa, Player holed out five consecutive bunker shots and lipped out a sixth, while demonstrating the explosion shot at the practice green 25 feet away.

Jimmy Demaret's chances in the 1947 Masters looked as if they were all wet until he pulled off one of the greatest escapes in tournament history. Demaret's ball was totally submerged in the water in front of the 15th green, but he hit an explosion shot that came to rest within four feet of the pin and made the putt for birdie. He went on to win the tournament.

At the International Tournament at Castle Pines Golf Club outside Denver in 1990, two pros had double eagles during the final round—the only known occurrence of such an event.

Steve Pate and Jim Gallagher Jr. both accomplished the feat on different holes.

At the 1998 Chick-fil-A Charity Championship, Sherri Turner scored a double-eagle 2 on the par-5 18th hole at Eagle's Landing Country Club in Stockbridge, Georgia. What made this amazing shot even more remarkable was that she had made an albatross at the very same hole in 1993. Tour officials believe she's the only person on a U.S. tour to ever double-eagle the same hole twice in competition.

In the fourth round of the 1954 Masters, Al Besselink hit his tee shot on the par-3 12th hole into the water. Miraculously, the ball landed on a small sandbar in midstream. Besselink waded out to the ball, pitched it onto the green, and then smoothed out the sandbar—just in case someone else might hit one there.

Remarkable Feats

In 1997, Tiger Woods shot a Masters record 70-66-65-69–270.
His 18-under-par total was one stroke better than previous
record holders Jack Nicklaus (1965) and Raymond Floyd
(1976). He also became the youngest Masters champion at 21
years, three months, 15 days. Woods's 12-stroke margin of
victory was the largest in tournament history.

In 1920, Ernest Jones, a Britisher who lost a leg in World War
I, once played the Clayton Golf Course in England without his
artificial limb. Jones, who became a professional golfer, shot a
par 72 by balancing on one leg.

Bert Yancey never came close to winning the Masters, but he did have a remarkable string of successes at the wicked over-the-water 190-yard 16th hole. Yancey made a birdie 2 eight times on that hole in nine consecutive rounds (all four rounds in 1967 and 1968, and in the first round of 1969). One reason for his success was that he constructed miniature models of the Augusta National greens so he could better understand their slopes.

Bobby Jacobson first won the championship of the Hollywood Golf Club in New York in 1932. By 1960, he had won the club title a remarkable 25 times. Only four other players ever managed to defeat him over that 29-year period.

Astonishing but True Golf Facts

Golf pundits were speculating that 38-year-old Arnold Palmer was washed up after missing the cut at the 1968 Masters, and finishing 59th at the U.S. Open. But then Palmer snapped an eight-month winless streak at the Kemper Open that year when he fired a final-round 67 to come from three shots back to win. Besides silencing his critics, Palmer reached a milestone. With the win, he became the first player to reach the $1 million career earnings mark.

Ten years before Casey Martin successfully sued golf over his right to ride, Charles Owens drew national attention to the plight of disabled golfers by playing nine grueling holes on crutches at the 1987 U.S. Senior Open. The Army vet, who blew out his knees in a 1953 paratrooping accident, got the support of Senator Bob Dole but was never allowed to ride. Still, he won two senior tournaments in 1986.

The longest drought between PGA victories belongs to Butch Baird. He waited 15 years, five months, and 10 days between wins at the 1961 Waco Turner Open and the 1976 San Antonio Texas Open. Ed Fiori waited long between wins too. His victory at the 1996 Quad City Classic was his first on Tour since the 1982 Bob Hope Desert Classic, a span of 14 years, eight months, and two days.

At Addington Palace in England, Ronald Jones performed a numerical marvel in 1934. He played a stretch of five holes like a man counting down for a rocket lift-off. On holes 12 through 16, he recorded scores, respectively, of 5-4-3-2-1.

Two threesomes who joined forces at the Mohawk Country Club in Tulsa, Oklahoma, in 1938 scored the 147-yard 4th hole in the following eerie fashion: 1-2-3-4-5-6. The ace was made by club pro Harold Nenninger, who then sat back and watched the amazing progression of the other scores.

The prolific James Robb of County Cork, Ireland, father of nine, accomplished an unusual feat on the links when he played his front nine at Portmarnock in 1941 in the ascending order of his children's ages. The feat, which Robb insisted was coincidental, began with an eagle 2 at the 1st hole and ended with a 10 at the 9th. The numbers: 2-4-4-5-6-7-8-9-10 for a total of 55.

The best round after a 400-mile cycle ride was posted by Donald Grant in 1939, who rode his bike from London to Royal Dornoch in the Scottish Highlands to play in the Open amateur. Grant tied for second place in the first round of the competition with a 74.

In the quarter-finals, the semi-finals, and the finals of the five United States Amateur championships won by Bobby Jones, he stood a total of 136 holes up on his 15 opponents. In other words, he won those 15 36-hole matches by an average of 9 and 8.

In 1988, LPGA player Mary Bea Porter was trying to qualify for a tournament at Moon Valley Country Club in Phoenix, Arizona, when she noticed three-year-old Jonathan Smucker was drowning in a nearby pool. She hopped a seven-foot fence and administered CPR until paramedics arrived. The boy made a full recovery. Meanwhile, Porter failed to shoot low enough to qualify after resuming her round, but the commissioner gave her a special exemption to play.

Greg Norman has done some astounding things on the golf course, but none as amazing as the time he told a 17-year-old leukemia patient that he would win a tournament for him— and then did it. Norman won the 1988 MCI Heritage Classic for Jamie Hutton, who had met Norman through the "Thursday's Child" Make-A-Wish program.

Babe Didrikson Zaharias was legendary for her competitive spirit and toughness, but she outdid herself when she played tournament golf a mere four months after abdominal surgery for cancer in 1953. She won five tournaments in 1954, including her third U.S. Women's Open.

In 1957, Doug Ford made a psychic prediction that would have amazed even the great Nostradamus. While entering a contest to name the Masters champion and his total score, Ford forecast himself as the winner and predicted 282 as his winning total. Weeks later, Ford not only won the 1957 Masters, but he did by shooting 282!

Astonishing but True Golf Facts

The greatest match-play golfer in history was probably Walter Hagen, who won the PGA Championship a record five times under that format and had an unbelievable string of 22 consecutive victories in matches from 1924 to 1927.

Tommy Armour lost almost all the sight in one eye after he was wounded in World War I. But the Silver Scot went on to win the 1927 U.S. Open and the 1930 PGA Championship, and then followed those wins with a very successful career as a golf instructor.

David Duval became the first player in PGA Tour history to win his first three career victories in consecutive starts when he caught fire at the end of 1997 and blazed through the Kingsmill, Disney, and the Tour Championship tournaments. Prior to pulling off his trifecta of titles, Duval had shown no sign of such ability—entering 86 events and winning none.

It was hail Irwin in 1997, when Hale Irwin collected $195,000 for winning the Boone Valley Classic in Augusta, Missouri—and in doing so broke the Senior Tour single-season earnings record before a hometown crowd. It so happened that he became the first golfer—at any level—to top the $2 million mark for one year.

In 1997, versatile Marty Joyce became the first man to qualify for the finals of the Remax North American Long Driving Championship in both the right-handed and left-handed categories. The 46-year-old teaching professional at Fresh Meadows Golf Course in Hillside, Illinois, qualified in the senior division with drives of 358 yards right-handed and 285 yards left-handed.

In 1997, LPGA pro Alice Miller completed the final round of the Welch's/Circle K Championship in a breathless record-setting time of one hour, 26 minutes, and 44 seconds. Because she teed off first and wasn't slowed by a playing partner, Miller cruised the course in overdrive. She also handled equipment cleaning and many other tasks normally performed by a caddie. The hurried pace didn't hurt Miller's game. She shot a slick one-under 71 for the round.

LPGA pro Laura Davies captured a piece of history in 1997 when she defeated Kelly Robbins at the Standard Register

Ping. The victory assured Davies a special place in golf history because she became the first-ever LPGA player to win the same tournament four straight years. The only two golfers to have done that so far are Walter Hagen (1924–27, PGA) and Gene Sarazen (1926, 1928–30, Miami Open).

Over the final few holes of the 1977 U.S. Open, the thought of sudden death weighed heavily on the mind of eventual champion Hubert Green. The golfer displayed plenty of guts just by completing, let alone winning, the tournament. Green managed to keep his composure after being informed that some nut had made a threat on his life. Said USGA official Sandy Tatum: "If courage is grace under pressure, then no one has more courage than Hubert Green."

Raymond Russell tied a European Tour record by birdieing the first eight holes at the One 2 One British Masters in 1997. After breaking the streak with a double bogey on the 9th hole, Russell bounced right back with a birdie on the 10th. The "one-under wonder" finished his record-setting round with a 64.

Weakened by tuberculosis and nearly fainting several times during the last round, Harry Vardon nevertheless won his fourth British Open title in 1903. After the victory, Vardon entered a sanitarium, made a complete recovery, and won two more Opens, in 1911 and 1914.

In 1953, Ben Hogan played in only six tournaments and, amazingly, won five of them. His wins included the Masters and the U.S. and British Opens. He took a pass on the PGA

Championship, which would have made him the first man to win the modern Grand Slam in the same year.

If birdies and eagles seemed as if they were drawn to John Huston at the 1998 Hawaiian Open, it's because he was positively magnetic about his winning 28-under-par performance. He credited his record-setting feat to magnets he put in his mattress cover and his shoes. He was urged to do so by Bill Roper, president of Tectonic Magnets, who said the devices could ease pain and aid circulation.

Talk about consistency and excellence. From 1962 to 1980, Jack Nicklaus finished third or better in 41 of the 76 major championships he entered. With such a tremendous stat—a 54 percent top-three ratio over 19 years—the Golden Bear deservedly made the short list of the 20th century's greatest golfers.

○

Between 1958 and 1978, Arnold Palmer, Jack Nicklaus, and Gary Player—the "Big Three" of modern golf—won 12 Masters, 8 British Opens, 7 PGA Championships, and 5 U.S. Opens for a total of 32 of those 84 modern major titles, an impressive .380 winning percentage.

○

In one 20-day span back in 1971, Lee Trevino won, in succession, three national titles in three countries: the U.S. Open, the Canadian Open, and the British Open.

Remarkable Feats

Californians Bob Aube and Phil Marrone went on a golfing safari in 1974. Determined to golf their way from Los Angeles to San Francisco, a distance of more than 500 miles, the pair made it in 16 days. They used more than 1,000 golf balls to cover the "course."

Before his death in 1970 at age 73, Joe Kirkwood had played more golf courses than anyone in history—in excess of 5,000! To put this feat in perspective, consider that the number two golf addict, Ralph Kennedy, played "only" 3,615 golf courses before his death in 1962.

Golf generally runs in families, but there has been only one father-and-son combination in the history of the Ryder Cup.

Englishmen Percy and Peter Alliss both made the team in their respective generations—Percy appeared four times (1929, 1933, 1935, and 1937) and Peter played in eight cups (1953, 1957, 1959, 1961, 1963, 1965, 1967, and 1969).

One of the biggest swings in the history of the Masters Tournament occurred in the final round in 1937, when Byron Nelson overtook the leader, Ralph Guldahl. Nelson played the 12th and 13th holes in birdie 2 and eagle 3 while Guldahl shot 5 and 6, a swing of six strokes in just two holes.

Between 1923 and 1930, the year he retired from tournament golf at age 28, Bobby Jones finished first or second in the U.S.

Open every year except 1927. He also won five U.S. amateurs, three British Opens, and a British Amateur.

To even out the field at the 1997 Chrysler-Plymouth Tournament of Champions, officials in Fort Lauderdale, Florida, asked local pro Annette DeLuca to play as Meg Mallon's "noncompeting marker." The overjoyed club pro jumped at the chance, then eagled the final hole to tally a respectable 75 for the round—a score that beat 15 other pros, including Mallon.

Three golfers have rallied from a record eight-stroke deficit in the final round of a PGA tournament since 1970. They are: Mark Lye, 1983 Bank of Boston; Hal Sutton, 1985 Memphis; and Chip Beck, 1990 Buick Open.

When LPGA Tour malcontents were griping in 1978 about Nancy Lopez getting all the press, JoAnne Carner advised them to "go out and beat her" so the reporters will stop writing about Lopez. But for five weeks in 1978, Nancy was unbeatable. She won five LPGA Tour events in a row, the first to pull off such a feat.

Australian Richard Cavander-Cole wore out eight pairs of shoes during a week-long 1,141-hole golfathon to raise money for cancer research in 1997. He beat a record that had stood for 17 years, one held by Steve Hylton at the Mason Rudolph Golf Club in Clarksville, Tennessee.

You might want to let Noel Hunt play through if you ever see him behind you. He holds the world record for the most balls hit in one hour, a whopping 1,536 range balls at Shrigley Hall, Pott Shrigley in Great Britain, in 1990.

Wendy Ward shattered the LPGA's all-time to-par scoring record when she shot a blistering 23-under 265 to win her first tour event, the 1997 Fieldcrest Cannon Classic in Cornelius, North Carolina. She made 24 birdies and only one bogey over four rounds of 66-65-64-70. Prior to her record-setting performance, Ward had broken 70 just five times in her previous 74 rounds—with no rounds lower than a 68.

It took Mark O'Meara more appearances—15—to win his first Masters than any other champion. Next is Billy Casper, who won in 1970 after 14 attempts at Augusta National. Others include: Ben Crenshaw, 1984, after 13; and Ray Floyd, 1976, after 12. Cary Middlecoff, Sam Snead, and Ben Hogan all needed 10 tries before winning the green jacket.

In 1998, Al and Brent Geiberger became the first father-son duo to play in a PGA Championship. Al, who won the title in 1966, missed the cut while Brent finished 25 strokes behind winner Vijay Singh.

Tiger Woods started the third round at the 1998 Masters by three-putting the first hole. It ended a remarkable Masters streak of 113 holes without a three putt, a streak that dated back to 1996.

Remarkable Feats

Famed women's golfer Joyce Wethered was 96 when she died in 1998. Her stylish and powerful play changed people's perceptions of women's golf. In 1937, she won 71 of 73 matches while capturing four British women's and five English women's titles. Bobby Jones once said Joyce had the best swing he'd ever seen. Incredibly, she had only one formal golf lesson in her entire life.

Southern Methodist University sophomore Nick Biesecker wasn't good enough to earn a spot on the school team that competed in an NCAA Championship Regional in 1997. So he shot a 67 in a local qualifier for the GTE Byron Nelson Classic and earned one of the four spots in the field.

Laurie Auchterlonie was the first player to break 80 in all four rounds of the U.S. Open in 1902. He won the event by shooting 307, six strokes better than his nearest competitor in the eighth year of the Open.

Jack Nicklaus holds the record for the most golf courses played in a single day by a pro golfer. In 1991, the Golden Bear played 18 holes at 18 different golf courses in eight hours and 40 minutes to raise money for charity. Nicklaus crisscrossed Palm Beach County, Florida, in a helicopter, playing one hole per course. He shot 73, which was par for the 18. The event raised $590,000.

Two golfers played five full rounds of golf in five different countries in one day! On June 12, 1992, Englishman Simon

Remarkable Feats

Clough and Australian Boris Janjic, both club pros in Belgium, played 18-hole rounds in France, Luxembourg, Germany, Holland, and Belgium. The 90 holes were walked briskly by the players who accomplished their amazing feat in 16 hours and 35 minutes. Clough and Janjic, who traveled 273 miles between the courses in a car, shot a combined score of 772.

In 1977, Bob Struble, 14, and his fellow golfing companion Mark Felger, 13, shot 90 and 103 respectively at the Cazenovia Golf Course in Buffalo, New York. So what's so remarkable about that? When they finished their rounds, the teens rushed to the weight scale in the clubhouse. Sure enough, each one had shot his exact weight.

Wacky Shots

Charlie Sifford doesn't relish memories of the day he sliced a shot into a crowd at the Quad Cities Open. The ball landed directly on top of a hot dog that had been dropped on the ground by a spectator. There were plenty of howls from the gallery as the embarrassed golfer wiped mustard and ketchup from the ball before taking his drop and continuing with the round.

In 1997, Bill Morse, a seven-handicap golfer from Hartford, Connecticut, celebrated his 51st birthday in a bizarre way. At Connecticut's Country Club of Farmington, Morse launched his ball from the 1st tee, and it came to rest in the cup at the 18th! The drive had sailed through the branches of a large spruce tree 50 yards away, then reversed directions when it

44

caromed off rocks near a cart path. The banged-up ball landed on the left front of the 18th green and rolled about 30 feet into the cup.

At the Los Angeles Open one year, Bob Geared badly sliced his tee shot. It bounced onto the road that ran along the course—and caromed up into the hands of a worker standing in the back of a moving vehicle. The man then heaved the ball back toward the course. Incredibly, the ball landed on the green and rolled into the cup. The golfer was about to give himself an ace when the rules committee forced him to play a provisional ball and add a penalty stroke to his scorecard.

In 1973, Ken Foster of Elie Golf Club in Scotland hit three wayward shots in a row toward the 18th green. The first went through a window in the clubhouse. The second and third balls went through the same hole in the window!

LPGA Hall of Famer JoAnne Carner won a tournament thanks to a smack in the mouth. In the 1977 Talk Tournament at Wykagyl Country Club in New Rochelle, New York, Carner was leading the field as she came to the final hole, a 510-yard par 5. She shanked her third shot and watched in horror as the ball struck a woman spectator right in the mouth. The ball bounced off the fan's face, landed on the green, hit the flagstick, and stopped 30 inches from the hole. Carner made her birdie to win the tourney—and then consoled the spectator, who, fortunately, wasn't seriously injured.

Wacky Shots

In the final round of the 1993 Southwestern Bell Colonial, pro golfer Fulton Allem clubbed a drive that struck a tree, lofted an approach shot that smacked into a rock wall, and hit another approach into a fan's folding chair. Despite his wild shots, Allem went on to win with a tournament record score of 264.

Roger Maltbie was locked in a playoff at the 1976 Memorial Tournament at Muirfield Village in Dublin, Ohio. During his four-hole playoff with Hale Irwin, Maltbie hit a shot that appeared to be heading off course. But his ball struck the out-of-bounds stake and rebounded toward the fairway. The lucky bounce helped him win the tourney. Maltbie carried the friendly stake around with him on the Tour for the rest of the year, but he finally left it under his bed in a motel room.

On the Links at Musselburgh, Scotland, in 1894, clubmaker Thomas Waggot played an entire round in which he teed off from the face of a pocket watch. Amazingly, the watch was undamaged at the end of play.

In the foursomes at the 1929 Ryder Cup at Moortown Golf club in Leeds, England, two-man teams played one ball and alternated shots. Joe Turnesa hooked his approach shot on the last hole behind the scoreboard at the green. Partner Johnny Farrell then pitched the ball over the sign to four feet, and Turnesa knocked in the putt to halve the match.

As a publicity stunt before the 1977 Lancome Trophy Tournament in Paris, Arnold Palmer hit three balls from the second stage of the Eiffel Tower, more than 300 feet above the ground. As Parisians craned their necks, Arnie cracked one drive 403 yards—and sent another one even farther when it hooked into an open-air double-decker bus and rode for an extra block.

In 1974, Nigel Denham was playing in the English Amateur Stroke Play competition at Moortown, Leeds, England, when he hit his ball past the l8th green and into the clubhouse. There was a local rule that the clubhouse was "in bounds." Playing the ball off the carpet in the clubhouse, Denham calmly chipped the ball out through an open window and scored a bogey 5.

Lucky bounces are all part of the game, but here's a sequence that defies belief: John Remington, playing England's Cotswald Hills Golf Club in 1959, took a five-iron at the short 7th hole and hooked it badly toward a drainage ditch. His ball caromed off a drainpipe toward a greenside bunker where it hit a rake and bounded toward a ball already on the green. Remington's ball glanced off the other ball and skipped into the cup for an ace!

In 1990, Bernhard Langer climbed 10 feet to the roof of a rain shelter in a tournament in South Africa to play his errant ball. He pitched the shot from its lofty lie to within three feet of the hole, and made the putt for a birdie.

In 1983, Canadian amateur golfer Elaine Johnson was shocked when her miss-hit ball landed in her own bra. "I'll take a two-stroke penalty," she said. "But I'll be damned if I'll play it where it lies."

In the first round of the 1952 Los Angeles Open, amateur Bud Hoelscher's approach shot to the 18th green hit a cameraman on the head, inflicting a scalp wound. The ball then bounced off a can of water, hit the greenside announcer in the face, and fell onto the green some 40 feet from the hole. Hoelscher then two-putted for a bloody par.

While walking on the course near his home at Knole, England, Ray Wickham was struck in the chest by a tee shot. He was unhurt and joined in the search for the ball, which couldn't be found—at least not until Wickham got home and discovered the ball . . . in his pocket.

A case of flag waving resulted in a birdie for Bobby Locke at the Irish Open in 1936. His tee shot at the 100-yard 12th hole appeared to be lost—until someone shook the flagstick. Locke's ball had become entangled in the flag. It then fell onto the green just inches from the hole.

In 1928 at Wentworth, England, playing partners Earl Avery and Richard Alcorn were on opposite sides of the fairway at the 9th hole when, unbeknownst to each other, they simultaneously struck their approach shots. The balls were heading toward the pin from different angles when they collided and plopped onto the green, inches from the cup.

Trick-shot artist and world-class amateur golfer E. T. Knapp gained notoriety for hitting an *eggstra-terrestrial* shot in 1901. He would drive a ball from the top of a hen's egg. The only crack Knapp made in the egg was a small dent from teeing up the ball.

In 1977, William Collins tried to hit his ball over a grapefruit tree at Eldorado Country Club in Palm Desert, California. He caught the shot a little thin and the ball went into the tree and disappeared. Upon further investigation, the ball was found— embedded in a grapefruit like a seed.

Astonishing but True Golf Facts

During a Royal and Ancient Tournament at St. Andrews, Scotland, in 1907, a member of the R&A drove a ball that struck the sharp point of a hatpin in the hat of a woman who was crossing the fairway. The ball was so firmly impaled on the pin that it stayed anchored to the woman's hat. The woman was unhurt.

Playing the 13th hole at Carnoustie, Scotland, in 1911, the Reverend A. R. Taylor saw his ball hit something in flight. It was another ball that had been launched from the 14th tee. Amazingly, each ball bounced directly back toward the player who hit it.

Joe Kirkwood, a legendary Australian trick-shot artist of the 1930s, used to tee a golf ball on the flat side of a Hershey's Kiss held between the teeth of an attractive female assistant. After whacking the drive, he would kiss his assistant, much to the delight of his audiences.

Jim Haderer, 16, of Elgin, Illinois, was so impressed by Paul Hahn's 1965 trick-shot performance at Elgin's Wing Park Course, he wanted to try one of Hahn's gags. So Hahn gave him a chance to play a shot from a kneeling position. On the first try, Haderer knocked his shot 190 yards right into the hole.

Peculiar Putting Facts

"Wild Bill" Mehlhorn claimed that he was the world's worst putter. One time when he was only 10 feet from the hole, he took six putts before holing out. Said Mehlhorn, "I never hit a careless one, except the sixth, and that was the one that went in."

Without any postal codes and marked with only the simple address "Misser of Short Putts, Prestwick," the British Post Office delivered a letter to its rightful recipient. It was Old Tom Morris, England's top golfer of the nineteenth century who sometimes suffered a bad case of the yips.

Peculiar Putting Facts

Jerry Barber put on one of the most remarkable putting performances in tournament play in near darkness during the 1961 PGA Championship. Barber was trailing Don January by four strokes with only three holes to play. But Barber sank successive putts of 22 feet, 44 feet, and 58 feet—two for birdies and one for par—to tie a stunned January. Then Barber beat him the next day in a playoff.

Leslie Balfour-Melville was a great golfer but a lousy putter in the old days at St. Andrews. He won the King William IV Medal no less than seven times and was the British Amateur champion in 1895. He played golf nearly every day of his life, well into his late 80s. When he died, he left a collection of more than 100 putters. It was said that his dying words were, "You know, I never *could* putt!"

In his prime, Bobby Jones used a putting stance with his feet no more than two or three inches apart. Sometimes his heels would actually touch each other.

George Low, professional putting teacher, recalled a sneaky tactic by golfers from the early days of the sport: "When they had a fast downhill putt, some of the old timers would spit on the ball to keep it from going too far."

Ben Hogan's hatred of putting—he once recommended that the stroke be completely eliminated from golf—stemmed in part from his finish at the 1946 Masters. There, he needed only par at the 18th hole to tie Herman Keiser, who had three-putted the hole. Hogan hit his approach shot to no more than 20 feet from the hole, but he three-putted to give Keiser the crown.

Peculiar Putting Facts

The yips began to strike Mac O'Grady shortly after the 1987 season when he earned a career-high $285,109 on the money list. The next year he dropped to $116,153 and then $40,090 in 1989, when he was 170th on the money list. He was so desperate to cure his crippling case of the yips he donated $30,000 to the medical department at UCLA to study the problem. A cure has yet to be found.

In one of the most atrocious putting performances ever, Brian Barnes took an incredible 12 strokes while putting from only three feet away from the cup at the 1968 French Open. On the 8th green, the short-tempered Barnes missed an easy putt. Then he tried to rake the ball in. When that failed, he hit the ball back and forth while it was still moving. Adding putts and penalty strokes, he scored a woeful 15 on the par-3 hole.

Astonishing but True Golf Facts

The average golfer who suffers from the yips is 45 years old and has been playing golf for 30 years. On average, the yips last for six years. Golfing greats who've been stricken with the yips include Ben Hogan, Johnny Miller, Orville Moody, Bernhard Langer, Sam Snead, and Tom Watson.

At the 1958 Lafayette Open, Tony Lema putted his ball *backward*—off the green and into a bunker. Lema's ball had sat precariously close to the edge of a sharply sloping ridge before the boner. While he was lining up the tough putt, Lema's club head accidentally tapped the ball backward, sending it down the slope and into a sand trap.

Alex Smith, U.S. Open Champion of 1906, was renowned as a rapid putter. He usually took less than 10 seconds to line up his putt and stroke it. His motto was: "Miss 'em quick."

Peculiar Putting Facts

Bobby Locke, the greatest putter in history, once went an entire season in 1948 without three-putting a single green in tournament competition.

Pro golfer Horton Smith claimed he faced some ridiculous putts in Scotland in 1964 because the wind blew him off balance at the moment he was starting his putting stroke. Because of the gusts, he blew easy putts from two to three feet away. But the crazy wind also helped him. "I remember one putt that went by the hole and the wind blew it back in," he said. "During the last two rounds I got down on my knees to putt so the wind wouldn't bother me so much."

Harry Vardon's name is on the trophy awarded to the player with the lowest stroke average each year. But Vardon himself took one wasted stroke in the 1900 U.S. Open, when he whiffed a putt that was shorter than six inches. He won anyway.

Once, after putting badly in the 1963 Walker Cup competition, Billy Joe Patton dashed to the Firth of Forth, the estuary next to the Old Course at St. Andrews. He hurled his putter far out into the water and yelled, "You'll never three-putt for me again!"

On his way to a convincing victory in the 1955 Masters, Cary Middlecoff sank what was one of the longest putts in Masters history. Cary was five under par when he came to the 480-yard, par-5 13th hole. His second shot, a three-wood, carried over Rae's Creek, but the ball rolled 85 feet beyond the cup. Despite the green's many undulations, Middlecoff sank the putt for an eagle 3. He finished at 279, nine under par, seven strokes ahead of Ben Hogan at 286.

In winning the 1920 English championship, famed golfer Joyce Wethered sank an eight-foot putt on the 17th hole to beat Cecil Leitch. As Wethered stroked the pressure putt, a train roared by in a track-rattling fury that shook the gallery but left her unfazed. When asked how she avoided the distraction of the locomotive, Wethered said, "What train?"

Astonishing but True Golf Facts

In the first round of the British Open in 1927, Bobby Jones needed only 28 putts. He never missed a putt under 12 feet—and six of them were from more than 100 feet! On the 5th hole, Jones sank a putt that was paced off at 120 feet.

What are the most putts ever taken on a single green? A. J. Lewis, playing at Peacehaven, Sussex, England, in 1890, reportedly needed 156 putts on one memorable hole.

The fifth hole at Augusta National is a 435-yard par 4 with an upper- and lower-level green that once sent Sam Snead on an emotional roller coaster. In 1954, Snead played his second shot to the right front of the green, leaving him about 40 feet from the cup, which was on the upper level. Snead's first putt just made it to the crest of the plateau, where it died momentarily, then turned left, and inched its way back down to the lower level about 10 feet farther away than it was when he started. So what did a seemingly crushed Snead do? He holed his second putt! Snead said later that it was one of the greatest two-putts he ever made.

The expression to "whiff" the ball originated in 1876, when Lord Gormley Whiffle completely missed a four-inch putt to lose the Silver Medal at St. Andrews's Old Course. The spectators kept remarking to one another, "Did you see that Whiffle?" Later the phrase was shortened to its present form.

Ben Sayers never won the British Open, but competed in it every year from 1880 to 1923. Whenever he sank a putt, he would celebrate by turning cartwheels on the green. Sayers had been trained as an acrobat.

Chick Evans never dreamed it would take him six strokes to hole out from 15 feet away at the 1921 U.S. Amateur. His first putt skipped four feet past the hole; the return putt also missed. The disgusted Evans then putted one-handed. When he saw his ball was again off-line, he swung and hit it again while it was still rolling—an automatic two-stroke penalty. Evans cooled down and then finally holed out.

Hale Irwin blew a two-inch tap-in at the third round of the 1983 British Open at Royal Birkdale that cost him a chance at a playoff for the championship. A 25-foot birdie putt at the 198-yard, par-3 14th came to rest just two inches past the cup.

Peculiar Putting Facts

Amazingly, Irwin whiffed the gimme and eventually finished in a tie for second, one stroke from a playoff with Tom Watson.

It took golfer Kim Saka 25 minutes to sink a simple 18-inch putt, all because of an ornery flagstick. Saka, an amateur from Mesa Verde, California, knew she would qualify for the 1980 Women's Kemper Open if she made the short putt on the final hole. But no matter how hard the caddie tried, he couldn't get the flagstick out of the hole. He tugged and tugged to no avail. Finally, after several caddies battled the stubborn stick for nearly half an hour, the pole was freed. Saka then sank the putt that put her in the tourney.

Jimmy Hines—always a contender but never a national champion in the 1930s—had a chance to beat Sam Snead in the 1938 PGA Championship. Hines was one up at the 14th hole when Snead's putt stopped 18 inches from the cup in perfect line with Hines's ball, which was three feet away. (They didn't pick up the ball and mark it in those days.) "I hit a perfect niblick over his ball and my ball went into the cup," Hines recalled. "Unfortunately, it ticked Sam's ball and caused his to start rolling right into the cup too. I lost the match, one down."

Mark Calcavecchia had a tremendously long putt over a huge mound on one of the large greens at St. Andrews, Scotland, during the 1990 Dunhill Cup competition. So rather than putt, he took out his wedge and pitched the ball to within a few feet from the hole. The gallery was horrified at the size of the divot Calcavecchia took out of the green, but he didn't mind. He then pulled out his putter and tapped the ball into the hole for a par.

Incredible Aces

The first known hole in one in a tournament was made in 1868 at the Open Championship at Prestwick, Scotland. Young Tom Morris scored the ace on the 145-yard 8th hole. Although there may have been earlier holes in one, this was the first to be recorded. Young Tom went on to win the tournament, his first of four victories in a row.

In one of the most amazing feats in golf history, four players aced the same hole during the same round of the 1989 U.S. Open. Mark Wiebe, Jerry Pate, Nick Price, and Doug Weaver all used seven-irons to knock their tee shots into the cup on the 167-yard 6th hole at Oak Hill Country Club in Rochester, New York. The odds of this happening are one in 8,675,083.

Astonishing but True Golf Facts

Successive holes in one on par-3 holes are rare, but they are
nearly unheard of on par-4 holes. Nevertheless, Norman Manley
pulled off this feat in 1964 at Del Valley Country Club in
Saugus, California, when he aced the 330-yard 7th hole and the
290-yard 8th hole. He shot 61 for the round, a course record.

Suzan Toft, 72, and Gill Dyke, 62, were playing in a foursome
when both aced the 116-yard par 3 at England's Trentham
course in 1997. A local TV station got word of the feat and
asked the ladies to replay their shots for the camera. Incredibly,
Toft sank her five-wood tee shot again! However, the pressure
was too great for Dyke, who failed to copy her partner a second
time.

During a shotgun start at the Highland Golf Club in
Cosmopolis, Washington, Bob LaCroix teed off on the par-3

15th hole. His tee shot ricocheted off a tree—and plopped right into the hole for an ace just 10 seconds after the gun had gone off.

Jim Whelehan, a Rochester, New York, phone company executive, had two aces on the same hole on the same day. In 1992, Whelehan played an 18-hole round in the morning and aced the 155-yard, par-3 4th hole at Heather Glen Golf Links in Myrtle Beach, South Carolina. Later that day in a second round, Whelehan repeated the feat: same ball, same hole, same result.

There couldn't have been much luck left in the Sacramento area in 1997 after Jeanette Roberts got done golfing. The 49-year-old 35 handicapper made an amazing three aces in five rounds at the Granite Bay Golf Club. Mathematician Wally

Astonishing but True Golf Facts

Etterbeek of Cal State–Sacramento said for you to match her feat, you would have to hit one shot on a par-3 hole every minute of every hour of every day—for 5,700 years.

Three generations of the Fribley family have all aced the 186-yard 7th hole at the Pana Country Club in Pana, Illinois. First, John Fribley scored a hole in one with a three-wood in 1971. Four years later, his teenage grandson, Scott Fribley, duplicated the feat. Finally, in 1992, Judge Joseph Fribley, John's son, became the third member of the Fribley family to ace the seventh hole.

In 1987, William J. Kirn struck his seven-iron toward the water at the par-3 3rd hole at the Kiahuna Golf Club in Koloa,

Hawaii. Kirn's ball bounded off a rock in the middle of the water, shot 25 feet into the air, drifted to the left, and landed on the green—where it rolled another 20 feet right into the hole!

In 1992, amateur J. T. Ward scored a hole in one—with his putter. He used a putter with a six-inch-long head that he claimed allowed him to hit the ball straighter than his other irons. Ward teed off with his putter at the 177-yard 3rd hole at Yarborough Landing Golf Course in Ashdown, Arkansas, and made his amazing ace.

In 1991, at the hilly 127-yard 5th hole of the Fountain Grove Country Club in Santa Rosa, California, John Gentile had some doubts about whether he'd find his wayward tee shot. So he played a provisional ball—right into the cup. Instead of an ace, he had scored a 3. Two weeks later, Gentile topped a drive at the 171-yard 12th hole at the same country club. So he decided to hit a mulligan. Incredibly, his second tee shot found the hole. Said Gentile, "It's hard being known as the guy who can't do it right on the first shot."

At the Singapore Open in 1981, a special cash prize of $50,000 and a $40,000 car were offered to anyone who aced the 17th hole. Amateur Yoshiaka Ono, 25, scored a hole in one. But then he realized that if he accepted the prizes, he would lose his amateur standing. Ono sat in the locker room, head in hand, for three hours, mulling over whether to turn pro. Finally he stood up and announced, "I don't want to be a professional, but I'll never forget Singapore."

The members of Baltusrol Golf Club complained that Robert Trent Jones, course designer, had made the par-3, 194-yard 4th hole too demanding for the 1954 U.S. Open. So Jones, escorted by the club pro and club president, went out to the 4th tee—and proceeded to knock the ball into the cup for an ace! Then he said, "As you can see, the hole really isn't too difficult."

Astonishing but True Golf Facts

At Vestavia Country Club in Birmingham, Alabama, Don Wendling made two holes in one in one week—both times shooting better than his age by three strokes. In 1998 Wendling, 82, sank a five-wood on the 200-yard 10th hole, then four days later drained a seven-iron on the 140-yard 14th. The latter ace was especially satisfying because the hole was named for the late blind golfer Charley Boswell, a good friend of Wendling's.

In 1998, five-year-old Matthew Stuart was golfing for only the fourth time in his short life when he scored an ace from the ladies' tee at the 86-yard, par-3 7th hole at Fox Ridge Country Club in Washington, Indiana. His father, Troy, said the youngster was excited, but after the round the boy immediately resumed playing with his toys.

Incredible Aces

George and Margaret Holmes had been married for over 50 years without notching a hole in one until two special days in 1997. It was ladies first as Margaret made her ace on the 130-yard 13th hole of the Holmeses home course of Grosse Ile Golf and Country Club in Michigan. The very next day, George hit his first hole in one at the 170-yard 6th hole.

In 1990, identical twins Barry and Jody Wolfe, 15, each aced the 2nd hole at the Scott County Park Course in Gate City, Virginia. First, Barry holed his six-iron tee shot. Then Jody, also using a six-iron, smacked his shot into the hole, right on top of his brother's ball! It was the first ace for each of the Wolfe boys, both 16 handicappers at the time.

Astonishing but True Golf Facts

"This is totally rad!" were the first words 14-year-old Kyle Davis exclaimed after he sank not one, but *two* aces during a single round at his hometown course, the Royal Oak Country Club in Greenwood, Indiana, in 1997. The amazing eighth grader grabbed his first hole in one on the 159-yard 3rd hole with his six-iron, then déjà vued the feat with a three-iron ace on the 160-yard 8th hole.

The number 17 was especially lucky one day in 1920 at the Coombe Hill Golf Course in Surrey, England. Alex Herd, famous British champion, made his 17th career ace—on the 17th hole. Moments later, on the same hole, Herd let a friend borrow the five-iron with which he had scored the hole in one. The friend promptly drove his tee shot smack dab into the cup for another ace on the 17th.

Incredible Aces

Father William Buckley, an Irish priest who was home on vacation from South Africa, played at Ballybunion in Ireland in 1971 with Father Ted Molyneux, and aced the 8th hole. Father Buckley came back again two years later and played with Father Molyneux—and scored another ace at the 8th hole!

Avid golfer Cy Hulsebus played the game for 60 years without experiencing the thrill of making a hole in one. Then in 1996, the 75-year-old Carroll, Iowa, man made up for lost time by nailing not one but three aces at the Carroll Country Club. Never-say-die Cy tallied his triple play of holes in one with his seven-iron.

In 1998, Chris Baird of Greensburg, Pennsylvania, hit a six-iron tee shot out of bounds on the 179-yard 6th hole at

Pleasant Valley Country Club in nearby Bullskin Township. Reloading after taking his penalty strokes, he socked the next ball right in the cup for a hole in three. Incredibly, he had done the exact same thing—made a three on an ace—on the very same hole 10 years earlier.

Hoolie White doesn't remember whether Franklin Roosevelt or Harry Truman was president when he made his first hole in one at the 139-yard 6th hole at the Anson (Texas) Golf Course. But in 1997, with one swing of his five-wood, the 91-year-old golfer became living proof that those who don't remember the past are doomed to repeat it. White not only picked up his second-ever ace, but he did so on the very same hole as his first more than 50 years earlier!

Incredible Aces

It took Jenny Lidback eight years and 190 tournaments to score her first hole in one in 1997. But then lucky Lidback seized the moment at the 1997 Chrysler-Plymouth Tournament of Champions and became only the second LPGA professional to record two aces in one event. The only other time lightning like this struck twice was at the 1979 Women's Kemper Open, when Jo Ann Washam sank two holes in one.

The longest hole in one ever recorded was by Lee Bruce in 1962 at the 480-yard dogleg 5th hole at Hope Country Club in Arizona. The record for women has stood even longer. Marie Robie knocked in a 393-yard ace at the Furnace Brook Club in Wollaston, Massachusetts, in 1949.

Astonishing but True Golf Facts

Golfers in America dream of the day when they get to mark an ace on their scorecard. Japanese save for it. In that tradition-bound, golf-crazy country, custom calls for players who score an ace to buy each of the witnesses an expensive gift, offer drinks for the entire clubhouse, and plant a tree commemorating the event somewhere near the green where the feat was done.

Nancy Bachand got a $150 check when Todd Obuchowski scored his first hole in one in 1998. Obuchowski, a 34-year-old sheet metal worker, sculled his tee shot on the 116-yard, par-3 4th hole at the Beaver Brook Golf Course in Haydenville, Massachusetts. It hit Bachand's passing Toyota, bounced back on the course, rolled onto the green and into the cup for an ace. At least eight players witnessed the freak shot. Obuchowski gratefully paid for the dent in the car.

Incredible Aces

Cecil Harwell of Bessemer, Alabama, scored two aces in
1986—one left-handed and one right-handed. His first ace on
the 155-yard 17th hole at Green Island Country Club came
left-handed with a seven-wood. Several months later, Harwell
played the hole right-handed, using a three-iron, and recorded
ace number two. The 76-year-old Harwell, an eight
handicapper, carried both left- and right-handed clubs. "It
really pays off when I come to a tree," said Harwell, who
learned to switch-hit by playing baseball.

England's Ian Garbutt lost $100 playing blackjack at the
Burswood Casino in Australia, but no one could call him a
loser. Shortly after his card-playing woes, he scored a timely ace
at the 16th hole at the Heineken Classic and won $100,000.
Not wanting to risk the loot at the gaming tables, he used the
money to buy a new house.

Astonishing but True Golf Facts

Bill Carey's haste cost him dearly one July evening in 1964. Carey hit his tee shot to the short 7th green at Roehampton, England, in the dying light, but couldn't find his ball. After a short search, he conceded the hole to his opponent, whose ball was hanging on the lip. After the concession, his opponent found Carey's ball—in the hole!

As great as Walter Hagen was, he scored only one hole in one in his life. It happened at the Worcester (Massachusetts) Country Club in 1926. On a 165-yard hole, Hagen used a one-iron to record his "1" with a ball marked "1."

John Murphy holed his tee shot at the 175-yard 5th hole at the Wil-Mar Golf Club in Raleigh, North Carolina, in 1982. But because he was playing alone, the unwitnessed ace was not official. After he had finished his round, Murphy took Hank Grady, the assistant greenskeeper, to the 5th hole, teed up another ball—and whacked it right into the cup! But because Murphy didn't hit this ace during an official round, this one didn't count either.

About the only thing Elaine and Dick Sauers had to fight about on a memorable day in 1998 at the Wolferts Roost Country Club in Albany, New York, was who would pick up the dinner check. Elaine used a seven-wood to ace the 10th hole from the 155-yard ladies' tee for her first hole in one. She carded the ace just three hours after her husband Dick had done it on the same hole with a six-iron from 166 yards out.

Astonishing but True Golf Facts

Amateur Joe Graney of Stuart, Florida, had cataract surgery on his right eye in 1992. Six days later, Graney scored his first hole in one on the 110-yard, par-3 11th hole at Heritage Ridge Golf Course in his hometown. A few months later, he had the other eye operated on. Incredibly, just six days later, he made another hole in one—this time on the 160-yard, par-3 7th hole.

In 1987, Walter Dietz scored his first hole in one on the 155-yard 7th hole of the Manakiki Golf Course near Los Angeles. What made it so remarkable was that Dietz was blind. "I played that course a thousand times when I could see," recalled Dietz. "The first time I played it as a blind person, I got a hole in one."

Strange Penalties and Rules

A weird sequence of rules violations highlighted a playoff at the 1991 Ben Hogan Reno Open. Marking his ball before a par putt, John Flannery moved his coin a putterhead-length away from Esteban Toledo's line. Toledo then missed his par putt, after which Flannery sank his par putt for an apparent win. But Flannery hadn't replaced his ball in the correct spot, so he was penalized two strokes. Meanwhile, Toledo, thinking he had lost, had his caddie pick up his ball marker. For not finishing the hole, Toledo was penalized one stroke. As a result, the hole was halved with double bogeys. However, Flannery won the tournament with a penalty-free par on the next extra hole.

Astonishing but True Golf Facts

One of golf's cruelest losses occurred in the 1968 Masters when Roberto de Vicenzo's playing partner, Tommy Aaron, incorrectly marked a 4 instead of a 3 on de Vicenzo's scorecard, costing the Argentinean a chance at a playoff with eventual winner Bob Goalby. Aaron's gaffe led to a joke that soon made its way to bars and clubhouses all over the country. Q: "What's the free drink some bars serve after you've paid for three?" A: "A Tommy Aaron—because it's the fourth shot you didn't ask for."

Bob Murphy was making a serious charge at leader Jack Nicklaus during the final round of the 1996 GTE Suncoast Classic. But Murphy muffed his shot at glory when he was hit with a two-stroke penalty—because a drive of his ricocheted off the lip of a bunker and conked him on his trademark hat. The poorly timed penalty put him out of contention.

Strange Penalties and Rules

Clowning around on a gimme putt, Andy Bean violated the rules by knocking the ball in with the grip, not the head of the putter, during the third round of the 1983 Canadian Open. He was assessed a two-stroke penalty that later came back to haunt him when he missed a chance at a playoff—by two strokes.

Don January set the unofficial record for loitering on a green at the final hole of the 1963 Phoenix Open when he waited a full seven minutes, hoping his teetering ball would drop into the cup. The ball never fell. Instead, the January Rule arose, stating a player has 10 seconds to tap his ball or face a penalty stroke.

He who hesitates loses. At least that variation of the old theme is what happened to golfer Denis Watson in the 1985 Open at

Oakland Hills near Detroit. Watson was cruising along in contention, when he waited too long for a putt to drop on a hole. After exceeding what official Monford T. Johnson thought was a "reasonable time," Watson was assessed a penalty stoke. He finished one shot behind Andy North, the eventual winner.

Early in his career, when he had yet to win any money, Ben Hogan was close to the lead on the final day of the 1943 Jacksonville Open. He putted to a flagstick being held by his caddie. The caddie tried to pull the pin out, but the liner of the cup came out instead, and the ball struck it. Hogan suffered a one-stroke penalty and was almost in tears when he eventually lost. His playing companion, Horton Smith, consoled him by saying, "Don't worry, Ben, you'll win someday!"

Fashion-conscious Swedish golfer Jarmo Sandelin went too far in his selection of golf attire, according to the PGA European Tour. It prohibited him from wearing transparent golf shirts. "I respect the decision," said Sandelin. "Nobody wants to see my nipples, do they?"

Astonishing but True Golf Facts

A two-stroke penalty was especially embarrassing for Tom Watson during the 1980 Tournament of Champions in Carlsbad, California. Watson forgot he had broken the rules when he gave advice to Lee Trevino during the match. Watson won the tourney by three strokes but was still red-faced because months earlier he'd published a book entitled *The Rules of Golf Explained and Illustrated*.

A string of 838 consecutive tournament starts without a disqualification ended for LPGA pro Kathy Whitworth in 1996. The Hall of Famer was heaved from the Chrysler-Plymouth Tournament of Champions for signing an incorrect scorecard.

During the 1992 Greater Greensboro Open, golfer Chip Beck unthinkingly pulled an out-of-bounds marker from the ground while lining up his next shot. His actions cost him a two-stroke penalty—and plenty of money. Because of the infraction, Beck finished in a tie for third. Without it, he would have ended up in second place by himself—a difference in earnings of a whopping $81,563.

Hawaiian-born Jackie Pung was accepting congratulations for winning the 1957 U.S. Open and its $1,800 first-place purse when the word came that she'd been disqualified. Pung burst into tears upon learning she had signed an erroneous scorecard. Members of the Winged Foot Golf Club in Mamaroneck, New York, felt so sorry for her that they raised $3,000 to ease her pain.

Craig Stadler saved himself a five-dollar laundry bill, but it cost him a disqualification and over $37,000 in prize money at the 1987 Andy Williams Open. To play his ball underneath a pine tree in a muddy lie, Stadler had to kneel. Not wanting to dirty his pants, he knelt on a towel and made his shot. By the time Stadler was notified that he had illegally built a stance and should have given himself a two-stroke penalty, he had signed and handed in an incorrect scorecard and was disqualified.

Leading the field after two rounds of the 1975 Dunlop Masters, Graham Marsh discovered to his horror that he had returned a scorecard with the wrong scores on two holes. Although his total score was correct, the fact that one hole showed a score lower than actually taken meant Marsh was disqualified.

Strange Penalties and Rules

It's a two-stroke penalty to touch any impediments in a hazard, but sometimes players forget where they are. Like Steve Elkington, who was waiting for a ruling at a tournament in Sweden in 1990. Bored with the wait, he reached down and pulled out a blade of grass to chew on. That cost him two strokes, which translated into the loss of $5,000 when the tournament was over.

The good folks at the USGA are not into hitting tee shots from their knees in the U.S. Open. In 1978, Bobby Clampett, playing as a marker, was asked to leave the course when he was observed light-heartedly hitting a tee shot—which traveled about 220 yards—from a kneeling position.

Astonishing but True Golf Facts

At the 1979 U.S. Open at the Inverness Club in Toledo, Ohio, the USGA was appalled that golfer Lon Hinkle had found a significant shortcut for playing the par-5 8th hole—by deliberately hitting to the 17th fairway. Overnight, the officials planted a 24-foot Black Hills spruce to try to block any further such shots. It failed, but it did inject some humor into a rather dull Open.

During the second round of the 1977 Hartford Open, George Burns and Frank Beard were waiting on the 2nd hole when Beard took a few swings with one of Burns's new irons. Beard said, "George, these grooves look awfully big." Burns had the irons checked. The grooves were too wide and he was disqualified.

In the 1968 Schweppes Championship, Brian Bamford made the critical mistake of tarrying too long searching for his ball. After exceeding the five-minute limit, he found the ball and played the shot. Bamford came in with a 68 that would have led the field, only to learn he had been disqualified for looking too long.

Gary Smith didn't think there was anything wrong with his golf ball back in 1977 at the PGA Club Professional Championship, but he was very wrong. His ball didn't conform to the R&A specifications, and he achieved the dubious distinction of being the first player to get booted out of a national PGA event for teeing up an illegal ball.

Wendy Ward took a costly ride on a golf cart during the second round of the 1998 Office Depot tournament in Palm Beach,

Florida. A volunteer driving a cart marked "player shuttle" assured Ward a cart ride to more quickly cover the lengthy distance between the 9th green and the 10th tee was legit. The volunteer was wrong. Officials assessed Ward two strokes, and she ended the tourney in a tie for third, five shots off the lead.

After being disqualified from the 1997 Edina Realty LPGA Classic for signing an incorrect scorecard, Dina Ammaccapane opted to spend the final round in the cushy comfort of her hotel room rather than watch her sister, Danielle, compete. Somewhere between room service and pay-per-view, Dina called the course and found out Danielle had ended a five-year winless streak by winning the tournament.

Strange Penalties and Rules

Don't ever ask Mac O'Grady to keep your score. He made so many errors on Paul Azinger's scorecard at the 1997 Buick Classic that Azinger became distracted trying to make the proper corrections—all six of them. As a result, Azinger simply forgot to sign his card and was disqualified.

Lee Janzen was disqualified from the 1998 NEC World Series of Golf because of several alert TV viewers. During the first round, Janzen waited about 20 seconds before his ball, which was on the edge of the cup, fell into the hole. But TV viewers pointed out that Janzen took more than twice the 10 seconds allowed before his ball dropped. PGA officials watched the tape, agreed, and then disqualified Janzen for signing for a lower score than he actually had because he had failed to take a penalty stroke.

P. H. Horgan III shot a one-under-par 71 in the opening round of the 1998 Buick Open, but it didn't count. He had forgotten to register for the event and was disqualified after 18 holes. "I messed up," Horgan said. "We have to sign a bunch of forms and stuff when we arrive at any tournament and I just forgot."

Should a golfer be charged with a stroke if, while in the midst of his swing, he changes his original intent and hits at a snake that had slithered through his stance? In 1986, the Rules Committee of the Royal & Ancient Golf Club ruled "no stroke," citing a 1957 court decision in a suit involving escaped circus animals: "If a person wakes up in the middle of the night and finds an escaping tiger on top of his bed and suffers a heart attack, it would be nothing to the point that the intentions of the tiger were quite amiable." The committee decided that the principle must apply to snakes and swings as well.

Strange Penalties and Rules

Touring pro John McMullin was disqualified not once but twice during the first round of the 1960 Motor City Open. McMullin learned too late he'd assessed himself the wrong number of penalty strokes for taking a practice swing on the 7th hole—and for hitting his ball while it was still moving at the 14th. Each error called for an automatic DQ for McMullin because, by not adding the penalty strokes, he'd signed an incorrect scorecard.

The game of golf has been governed by 34 rules of play supported by 1,100 decisions based on actual golf situations. That's a far cry from the original 13 principles drafted by the Honorable Company of Edinburgh Golfers in 1744. Yet many people, including the late British golf journalist Henry Longhurst, campaigned to cut that number to a simple 10 rules that could be written out on a single index card. "The two most ghastly expressions in the English language are 'obtain relief' and 'send for a ruling,'" he once proclaimed.

Many pro golfers sport endorsement deals with clothing manufacturers. But not Robert Gamez, who showed up for the 1997 Canon Greater Hartford Open wearing a collarless shirt. While the PGA Tour does not have a specific dress code, the tourney was being played at the TPC course in River Heights, Connecticutt—and TPC had a rule that said, "No collarless shirts." Gamez was forced to buy a new shirt to compete.

Prior to losing a playoff to British Open winner Mark O'Meara in 1998, Brian Watts was losing a battle of patience with his hosts on the Japan PGA Tour. Watts was fined about $1,500 and banned from the 1998 Japan Open for deliberately hitting two balls out of bounds in a successful effort to miss the cut at the Fujisankei Classic. Watts, who later apologized to officials, claimed he was frustrated by his poor play.

In the playoff for the 1962 U.S. Open at Oakmont against Jack Nicklaus, Arnold Palmer missed a putt to give him a 74. He then picked up Nicklaus's ball and pitched it to him, conceding the tourney to the Golden Bear, who shot a 71. An alert official noted that in medal play, every hole must be completed—there are no concessions of putts. So Joe Dey, executive secretary of the USGA, escorted Nicklaus, who was in the scorer's tent, back to the green. The ball was placed at the spot from which it had been lifted, about 30 inches from the cup. Nicklaus then holed the putt and made his victory official.

When her tee shot at the par-3 13th hole of the 1993 NCAA Women's Championship splashed into the shallows of a lake, Holly Reynolds opted to play the ball where it lay. Holly's underwater whack nudged not only her ball up onto the bank but also a four-inch sunfish. After guiding the gaping guppy back into the lake, Holly got a sinking feeling she had committed an infraction. But USGA officials let the compassionate collegian off the hook because the rule book states only dead critters are considered "loose impediments"—obstacles that can't be moved.

Steve Melnyk discovered he didn't have the "write stuff" after flying 4,000 miles to play in the 1976 Hawaiian Open. Melnyk had made a verbal commitment to play, but when he arrived at the site officials wouldn't let him enter—because he hadn't given them advance written confirmation of his intent to play.

There was nothing Melnyk could do but mutter "Aloha" and fly back home.

According to the USGA, in 1997 a total of 13 rules workshops were held for players interested in learning the finer points of their craft. Notices were posted for players from the LPGA Tour, the PGA Tour, and the Senior PGA Tour. Only one player from all professional golf attended even one session: the LPGA's Annika Sorenstam.

While playing the Northern Telecom Open at Tucson National Golf Club in 1991, Hal Sutton drilled his six-iron second shot directly at the hole on the 9th green. The ball slammed into the cup without touching the green and embedded itself in the lip of the hole. Since part of the ball remained above the level of the hole, it was ruled that Sutton had not holed out. He had to replace the ball and putt it in for a birdie.

It was one small shot for man, one giant divot for mankind in 1970 when U.S. astronaut Alan Shepard used his six-iron to launch a few golf shots on the heavily cratered surface of the moon. In no time, members of one rules committee had cabled the man on the moon to advise Shepard of his responsibilities to the lunar surface. "Please refer to rules on golf etiquette, paragraph 6," read the cable. "Before leaving a bunker, a player should carefully fill up all holes made by him therein." The astronaut laughed it off as an act of lunar-cy.

Colin Montgomerie claims he bought his way out of a traffic ticket while speeding to the 1997 British Open. Stopped for doing 80 m.p.h. in a 30 m.p.h. zone, Montgomerie said he was given a mulligan by the police officer—after the golfer handed him a sleeve of golf balls.

Golfer Fred Hamilton gave new meaning to the term *cabin fever* in 1992 when he tunneled 32 feet beneath the walls of Moundsville State Penitentiary to play a round of golf. A convicted murderer, Hamilton was apprehended by an Oklahoma law man after a 12-state manhunt. Hamilton confessed that thoughts of golf had made him stir crazy. "He said he wanted to go to Pebble Beach and play golf," the officer reported.

Chicago-area golfers were wise not to bother duffer Vincent Gebhardi, otherwise known as Machine Gun Jack McGurn.

Astonishing but True Golf Facts

He was a mob hit man who helped gun down seven of Al
Capone's henchmen in the infamous 1929 St. Valentine's Day
Massacre. He was also a pro golfer who was once arrested on
the 7th hole at the Olympia Fields Country Club during the
1933 Western Open. Police let him finish his round, which
included a murderous 11 on the 8th. His 83-86 missed the cut
by 14 strokes.

Weird Injuries
and Mishaps

In 1975, Owen E. Cummings was playing the par-5 7th hole at a course in Fortville, Indiana. His second shot landed in four inches of water behind a stone wall. Cummings took a vicious swing and topped the ball. It ricocheted off the wall and bounded into the cup for an eagle 3. The shot won him the hole but cost him the match. When he swung, the club head struck the wall, flew off—and smacked Cummings in the face. He was carried off the course unconscious and unable to finish.

Martin Hardy of Southampton, England, was playing a round in Wales when he leaped up to see how he had fared with his shot from a bunker. As it turned out, he fared rather badly. At the top of his leap, he was struck in the head with a misdirected shot from one of his playing partners and was knocked unconscious.

On the 8th hole of the final round of the 1982 Greater Erie Charity Classic, Greg Powers had to play a shot from behind a tree with little room for his follow-through. When he tried to hit a three-iron, the club smacked into the tree. The shaft snapped and the club head whipped around, smacking Powers on the forehead. The blow was so hard it knocked him out for about five minutes. Despite the injury, Powers continued to play, holding an ice bag to his head between shots for the final 10 holes. Incredibly, he gained three shots on the field and finished with a 65 for fourth place in the tournament. Afterward, Powers went to the hospital where he was treated overnight for a concussion.

Weird Injuries and Mishaps

Hubie Smith, Tennessee's Senior PGA Player of the Year, was
declared the winner of the 1992 Harold Eller Pro-Am—while
lying flat on his back. Smith shot a leading score of 67 in the
first round of the two-day event. After his round, he suffered
chest pains caused by blockage in an artery and was
hospitalized. Fortunately for Smith, the second day was rained
out and he was declared the tournament champion. "It's the
first tournament I ever won from intensive care," Smith joked.

Before the third round of the 1998 Home Depot Invitational,
Doug Sanders spent three hours in the emergency room from a
severe nose bleed caused by an antihistamine. Despite being
weak and dizzy, Sanders golfed later that morning. Playing
partners Will Sowles and Orville Moody became concerned
when Sanders began staggering on the back nine. He insisted
on finishing, making two pars and a birdie before he was rushed

to the hospital for intravenous fluids and medication. Sanders was back on the tee Sunday morning and shot a 78.

"Champagne" Tony Lema became so excited after making a dazzling shot at the 9th hole of the 1957 Bing Crosby National Pro-Am that he leaped into the air. Pleasure turned to pain, though, when Lema tumbled over an 18-foot cliff and landed at the bottom. He suffered bruises to his shins, elbows—and ego.

Bill Glasson earned the 1997 Comeback Player of the Year award by enduring 13 surgeries and still managing to compete on the Tour. At the awards ceremony, however, he was given an ironically appropriate prize—a Waterford crystal bowl that accidentally was cracked.

Barbara Romack, 1964 U.S. Amateur champion, was invited to play golf in Palm Springs with former president Dwight Eisenhower and comedian Bob Hope. To her dismay, she shanked a shot that flew directly through the front of the cart carrying the president, narrowly missing him. Said a shaken Romack, "I came awfully close to being a presidential assassin."

Jerry LaCerra, an aspiring Italian opera singer, was practicing a few arias as he waited on a tee at the Naples Country Club in Naples, Italy, in 1952. His partners were chipping balls as they waited and one of them shanked a shot into the singer's open mouth. LaCerra suffered a chipped tooth.

Crazy bounces are all part of the game, as Jim Armstrong of Phoenix found out in 1963 when his tee shot hit a tee marker in front of him, bounced straight back, and hit him in the forehead. When he came to, Armstrong teed it up again and astonishingly hit another ball into the same marker. This time the ball bounced back and hit him in his kneecap. Armstrong then limped off the course.

Weird Injuries and Mishaps

Golf ordinarily isn't a contact sport, but you couldn't tell that to D. B. Hendry, a competitor in the McLeod Cup at Old Ranfurly in 1969. Hendry was standing on the 16th tee when an errant shot smacked him in the jaw and collarbone, knocking him unconscious. Disregarding a doctor's advice to retire, Hendry finished out the round with a 66 and followed it that afternoon with another 18-hole score of 70 to win the tournament in record fashion.

Real strokes of tragedy sometimes befall golfers. In the summer of 1963, Harold Kalles of Toronto, Canada, was mortally wounded when his throat was cut by a golf club shaft that broke against a tree as he was tying to play out of a bunker.

Pro golfer "Wild Bill" Mehlhorn felt dizzy from too much partying between the third and fourth rounds of the 1930 Western Open at Indianwood in Detroit. He fell down when he went to tee the ball up on the first hole, so he had his caddie tee it up for the rest of the round. Amazingly, Mehlhorn shot 33 on the front nine and came back in 32, for a five-under-par 65. He had eight birdies and an eagle, but it still wasn't enough for a win.

In 1951, Edward M. Harrison was playing alone at the Inglewood Country Club in Seattle when he apparently broke the shaft of his driver. The split shaft pierced his groin. He tried in vain to reach the clubhouse, finally collapsing and bleeding to death 100 yards from the 9th tee.

Weird Injuries and Mishaps

Mike Reasor holds the PGA Tour record for the highest 36-hole total ever recorded in the last two rounds of a tournament, and not because he played badly. Reasor made the cut in the 1974 Tallahassee Open, but then injured his left shoulder riding a horse. Because players who completed the tournament got an automatic entry into the next week's event, Reasor decided to finish, playing one-handed. In the final rounds, he shot 123-114.

Mark Calcavecchia nearly put himself out of contention at the 1998 Honda Classic with a nasty slice that happened miles from the course. He was cutting the tags off some new pants when his left index finger got in the way of the scissors. Luckily, his chiropractor, Al Jerome, was in the house and told him to Super Glue the wound. "An old Army trick," Jerome told the skeptical golfer. It worked, and Calc shot a 65 for a three-shot victory and $324,000 in prize money, enough for a lifetime supply of Super Glue.

Great shot! While taking a practice swing on a municipal course in Ohio in 1974, Bob Russell sent up a cloud of smoke and felt a searing pain in his leg. The club head had set off a .22 caliber bullet that somehow had been resting in the turf. Fortunately, Russell was merely grazed.

During the 1997 Buick Invitational, pro golfer Larry Silveira became angry in a local Laundromat when one of the washers wouldn't work even though he'd put enough coins into the slot. Frustrated, he slugged a nearby dryer with his fist and broke a bone in his hand, knocking him out of action for two months. It was only later he realized the washer was free.

Weird Injuries and Mishaps

Who says golf isn't a dangerous game? Loren Roberts broke two
ribs sneezing. The nose quake caused his earnings to nosedive
from $1,089,140 in 1997 to $210,247 in 1998. Still, in the
category of uncommon mishaps, Gary Player may have the
trophy. He once pulled a muscle while taking a bath.

Miguel Angel Jimenez held up play for about 15 minutes at
the 1998 Turespana Masters in Mallorca, Spain, when a painful
kidney stone forced him to go to the clubhouse for painkillers.
He returned to complete the round but officials warned him his
delay could lead to a two-shot penalty for slow play. He and his
partners ran the rest of the way until they caught up.
Amazingly, Jimenez survived the ordeal to win the tournament
with a nine-under 279.

Astonishing but True Golf Facts

The Tiger Woods phenomenon made for long lines at hospital emergency rooms in 1997 by beginners who were accidentally clubbing other beginners in the head. Dr. William Couldwell, chief of neurosurgery at Westchester Medical Center in Valhalla, New York, said he could not recall many golf-related injuries prior to Tiger, but since Woods's win at the 1997 Masters, nearly 30 percent of all operative trauma in children ages six to nine stemmed from being hit by a golf club.

In the 1974 Inter-Maritime Pro-Am at Divonne, France, one of the unfortunate amateurs lost more than a golf match. Marcel Dionne lost his entire set of clubs when his caddie, attempting to ford a stream swollen by rains, lost his balance and dumped the man's entire set of clubs in the river.

Weird Injuries and Mishaps

In 1975, Norman Anderson, well-known British amateur golfer, was furious at missing a putt at the Royal Bangkok Country Club in Thailand. In a rage, he flung his putter into the air. It struck a high-tension wire and completely disintegrated.

Giving new meaning to the phrase "it's in the cup," Leonard Crawley struck his shot to the 18th green in the 1932 Walker Cup matches just a little harder than he intended. The ball veered off the course. Then it hit, and dented, the Walker Cup, which was on display outside the clubhouse at the Country Club in Brookline, Massachusetts.

Golf and acting aren't always compatible. After winning the Oscar in 1944 for Best Supporting Actor for his role as the kindly priest in *Going My Way*, Barry Fitzgerald accidentally decapitated his prized trophy. He was practicing his golf swing in his house when he hit the wartime plaster statuette. Paramount paid $10 to replace it.

The gallery at the 1984 Memphis Classic saw more of Gary McCord than either they or he wanted when the golfer's pants split wide open. McCord turned the tourney into a skins game—because he wasn't wearing any underwear! Scampering for any kind of cover, McCord wrapped his caddie's towel around his waist, before finding another golfer willing to part with his rain pants—for a small fee of $20.

Here's a guy who really shot the lights out: J. D. Bryden was playing at Vertish Hill Golf Course in 1930 when his tee shot on the 2nd hole sliced onto the adjacent road and crashed into the headlamp of an oncoming car. The driver, apparently a golfer and definitely a sport, simply drove up to the tee and handed Bryden his ball.

Dreadful Golf Disasters
and Mental Miscues

Thirteen was the unluckiest number for Tommy Nakajima at the 1978 Masters when he tied a Masters record for the highest score on a single hole with a 13 on—what else?—the 13th. Nakajima, whose given name, "Tsuneyuki," means "always happy," was anything but splashing around in Rae's Creek. When reporters asked later what happened, they misunderstood his interpreter to say, "He lost confidence." What he really said, according to the interpreter, was "He lost count."

Tommy Armour III thought he had it made during the qualifying round of the 1983 Tournament Players

Championship. He reached the par-4 18th hole needing to shoot an easy eight or better to make the cut. But to his shock, he hit three straight drives into a lake and wound up with a disastrous nine on the hole—and missed the cut by one stroke.

The infamous pro Lefty Stackhouse blew his stack at a Texas tournament after driving six straight balls into a lake. Angry beyond belief, Stackhouse threw his club and entire golf bag into the water hazard. Then, when his caddie began to giggle, the peeved pro picked him up and tossed him into the lake too. To cap off his wet and wild tirade, the steamed Stackhouse cooled off—by diving into the drink after his equipment and caddie!

The highest score ever shot has probably never been recorded, but the late comedian Jimmy Durante may have been a challenger for that shameful honor. During his first-ever round of golf, Durante scored well over 200. "What shall I give the caddies?" Durante asked his playing partners following his marathon match. "Your clubs!" one of them shot back.

The first time Frank Sinatra played a round of golf with Arnold Palmer, Old Blue Eyes spent more time in the Palm Springs roughs than on the well-manicured fairways. After his horrendous round, Sinatra had the nerve to ask Palmer, "What do you think of my game?" The pro didn't bat an eye as he turned to his playing partner and said: "Not bad . . . But I still prefer golf."

Japanese golfer Tommy Nakajima was among the leaders at the 1978 British Open at St. Andrews until a 30-foot putt on the

17th hole rolled into the feared Road Bunker. A frustrated Nakajima needed four strokes to get his ball out of the deep bunker and back onto the green. After he scored a shocking nine on the hole, observers nicknamed the trap "The Sands of Nakajima."

No one quite let the PGA Championship slip through his hands the way Al Watrous did in 1932 at the Keller Golf Course in St. Paul, Minnesota. Watrous had been nine up with 12 holes to play, but Bobby Cruickshank had 11 one-putts over the final dozen holes to tie the match. In overtime, Watrous had a chance to win, but three-putted from only two feet away. That let Cruickshank tie him with a bogey 4. Given a reprieve, Cruickshank won the next hole, giving him the match and the championship.

When Tom Weiskopf knocked his ball into the pond five successive times at the 12th hole at Augusta National in the 1980 Masters, his wife, Jeannie, who was in the gallery, was in tears. A friend consoled her by saying, "Don't worry, Jeannie, Tom's not using new golf balls!"

In the 1920 British Open at Deal, England, George Duncan hit seven shots in a row out of bounds and then put his eighth on the green and holed out. Incredibly, he still won the tournament. At that time, the penalty for hitting a ball out of bounds was the loss of distance only.

While vacationing in Bermuda, Babe Ruth jumped at a chance to play on C. B. MacDonald's wonderfully designed Mid-Ocean

Club course. When he approached the elevated tee on the 370-yard 5th hole, Ruth asked for a driver. Being familiar with the course, his caddie suggested Ruth take the lake out of play and lay up. Ruth demanded the driver, saying, "I could throw it on the green from here." After sinking 15 balls in the water, Ruth snapped his driver over his knee and stormed back to the clubhouse.

John Ball Jr., the great amateur of Hoylake Golf Course in England, faced incredible adversity but refused to give up in the 1890 British Open. He landed in the notorious, huge, deep Half Moon Bunker at Prestwick Golf Course in Scotland. He needed 11 shots just to get out of the pit. Amazingly, despite the disastrous hole, Ball still managed to win the tournament by three shots.

Astonishing but True Golf Facts

Greg Norman has had one of the greatest careers in the history of golf. Still, many fans will most remember him for blowing a six-stroke lead to lose the 1996 Masters to Nick Faldo. Determined not to let it happen again in 1997, Norman sat down with motivational speaker Anthony Robbins. It didn't do much good. Norman shot 77-74 and did not make the cut. But then, neither did Faldo.

Scott Simpson and Olin Browne shared the dubious distinction of tying for the worst start in the history of the Masters. Both top money winners, they started the 1998 tournament with horrendous quadruple bogey 8s on the first hole. The previous high score had been 7, by 13 different unlucky players.

Arnold Palmer was leading Jack Nicklaus by a shot in the final round of the 1967 Bing Crosby Pro-Am at Pebble Beach when his tee shot on the 14th hole smacked a tree and bounced out of bounds. Palmer reteed his ball—and once again hit the same tree. Because of his disastrous encounter with the tree, Palmer lost the tournament to Nicklaus. But, with a little divine providence, Arnie's disappointment was somewhat assuaged. Late that night, a fierce storm uprooted the tree.

Ray Ainsley holds the record for the highest score ever on one hole at a major. During the second round of the 1938 U.S. Open at Cherry Hills Country Club in Denver, he shot an incredibly horrible 19 on the par-4 16th hole. After his approach landed in a fast-moving stream that fronted the green, he took off his shoes and socks and flailed away at his submerged ball. It took him 11 strokes to get it out of the water and another three to get it onto the green. Then he three-putted for his infamous 19.

Ralph Guldahl was the "Golden Boy" of golf in the mid-1930s. He won back-to-back U.S. Open championships in 1937 and 1938, as well as the Masters in 1939. Then, inexplicably, his swing deserted him. Guldahl played so poorly he left the pro tour and sold cars and real estate. The former champion never again recovered his masterful form.

Dreadful Golf Disasters and Mental Miscues

In one of golf's most embarrassing moments in international competition, Alvin Liau of Singapore, competing in the then-prestigious World Cup tournament in 1971, scored an 18 on the 13th hole at PGA National in Palm Beach Gardens, Florida, when he shanked six straight shots into a water hazard.

Dennis Murdoch occupies a low shelf in the lore of the British Open for his score on the 1st hole of the second round of the 1925 tournament. Murdoch shot a woeful 14 on the hole after airmailing the green with his approach shot, and then taking nine shots to get back on the course from a rocky path behind the hole.

Chevalier von Cittern compiled one of the sorriest average scores per hole of any golfer. Playing at Biarritz in 1888, von

Cittern shot 316 for 18 holes—an awful average of 17.55 strokes per hole.

In one of the most incredible collapses in Masters history, Jim Ferrier lost his six-shot lead over the final six holes in 1950, when he hit two balls into the water and shot five over par on the back nine. Meanwhile, Jimmy Demaret shot two under par over the same stretch to win the tourney by one stroke.

Watch your step! While on the green at the 1962 British Open at Troon, Max Faulkner carelessly tapped his foot against his ball and moved it for a one-stroke penalty. He became so unnerved by this event at the 11th hole that he ultimately required 11 strokes to hole out, carding a septuple bogey.

During the 1961 Los Angeles Open, Arnold Palmer was playing well in the first round—until the bottom fell out on the 508-yard, par-5 9th hole. The General then whacked four straight drives out of bounds and staggered to a horrendous 12 at the Rancho Park Golf Course, where a bronze plaque was later erected to commemorate Arnie's uncharacteristic crash.

Her playing partners might want to call her the Brink of disaster. Maria Brink drew the American Express Tour's 1997 Estroil Open to a grinding halt when she and her playing partners couldn't agree over how many balls she had shanked out of bounds. Tour director John Mort heard the argument and finally ruled she had whacked four balls out of bounds. Brink proceeded to make a routine two-putt for a 12.

Few golfers have gone over the edge quite like Jim Ferree, who tossed in more than the towel during the 1961 Canadian Open. Ferree was cursing his poor putting, a nagging backache, the awful weather, and fatigue when he stopped in the middle of a small bridge—and tossed his bag and clubs over the rail. When told he could face fines totaling $1,650, Ferree ordered his caddie to retrieve his gear and he continued with the match.

In the 1909 U.S. Open, David Hunter shot a 68, the first time anyone in that tournament had ever broken 70. Unfortunately, Hunter also established another first—the difficulty of following a low round in a major with another low round. The very next day, Hunter shot a miserable 84.

Golfers everywhere still shake their heads over the demise of the golden swing of Ian Baker-Finch, who carded a 29 on the back nine to win the 1991 British Open and then promptly lost his touch. But what's lesser known is that he won by two strokes over one-time leader Mike Harwood, who also went on to a future of professional golf anonymity.

Dave Bally landed his tee shot about 15 feet from the cup, yet he had the misfortune of taking a triple-bogey 6 on a par-3 hole at the 1988 Canadian Open. Bally was walking confidently toward his ball with putter in hand when he tripped. He watched horrified as his club struck the ball, sending it careening off the green and into a nearby pond.

After spending months of practice and raising thousands of dollars, Kansas City golfer Fred Rowland eagerly flew across the Atlantic to Wales to play in the 1988 British Amateur

Championship. But on the day of the biggest tournament of his life, Rowland was disqualified for missing his start—because he was still in the bathroom when he was called to the first tee!

It was three strikes and out of the money for Al Chandler at the 1986 Senior Tournament Players Championship. Chandler was battling Arnold Palmer for the lead when his ball dropped near a big tree on the 15th hole. Without much room for a back swing, Chandler tried to cut down his swing—and completely missed his ball twice before hitting it onto the green. His third whiff occurred on an easy putt and sent him tumbling to a thirty-second-place finish.

Despite his intellect, Jesper Parnevik has committed more than his share of bone-headed mistakes. He once lost his plane ticket four times—on the same trip. Even though he's a math wiz, he once miscalculated the cut that would have put him in a high-stakes playoff at the Sprint International in Castle Rock, Colorado. He drove to the airport while his opponents, fans, and tournament organizers scratched their heads on the tee waiting for Jesper.

Sam Snead did nothing more than stew for the nearly 30 minutes it took to clear the 18th fairway of fans during the 1939 U.S. Open at the Philadelphia Country Club. He could have used the time to ask where his competitors stood because there were no leader boards at the time. Mistakenly thinking he needed a birdie to win, Snead took several unnecessary chances and wound up with a disastrous eight on the final hole to finish fourth.

Astonishing but True Golf Facts

When Craig Stadler was a member of the University of Southern California golf team in 1975, he was late for a match against UCLA. Stadler sped to the course, jumped a hedge, and arrived at the first tee with seconds to spare. Unfortunately, he forgot his golf shoes. So Stadler played in the shoes he was wearing at the time—big, bulky desert boots. Incredibly, he hiked his way to a three-under 69.

When Tony Jacklin won the 1970 U.S. Open at Hazeltine, his prize money was $30,000 and the trophy. He took the check, endorsed it, and then absentmindedly left it in a trouser pocket when he sent his clothes to the cleaners. With the endorsement on it, the check was as good as cash. Fortunately, his laundryman was an honest person and returned the check to Jacklin.

Julius Boros learned never to take anything for granted. In the 1981 Doug Sanders Energy Classic in Houston, Boros finished his round early, several shots behind leader Art Wall, who was still out on the course. Figuring his day was over, Boros caught a plane and headed home early. But Wall faltered badly and finished behind the first-place scores of Billy Casper, Doug Ford—and Boros. So while Boros was winging his way home unaware of his first-place tie, Casper and Ford dueled in a playoff for the title.

At the age of 13, Jesper Parnevik confidently declared he would one day win the British Open. His prediction looked golden in 1994 until the final hole, when Jesper failed to look at the scoreboard. Needing only a par to win, Parnevik mistakenly thought he needed a birdie. Playing aggressively, he went for a birdie and wound up in the bunker, eventually making bogey and coming in second behind winner Nick Price.

Davis Love III thought he was all ready to play in the 1998 Nissan Open in Los Angeles. He had his airline ticket and a hotel reservation, and he'd even scheduled a round with a nine-year-old heart patient who was part of the Make-A-Wish Foundation. Davis told everyone—except the tournament organizers. Qualified tour players have to notify the tournament of their intention to play and Love did not do so and was disqualified. An embarrassed Love rescheduled the charity round.

Intriguing Facts About
Famous Golfers

The great Ben Hogan never forgot the turning point of his life. It happened in 1938 when he and his wife, Valerie, were down to their last $85. "If I didn't win money at the Oakland Open, I was through," Hogan recalled. "The night before the tournament started, someone stole the two rear wheels off my car. I had to hitch a ride to play. But I shot a 69 in the last round and tied for third. The $385 I won enabled me to put wheels back on my car and keep going." After that tourney, Hogan began winning with regularity.

Mac O'Grady began trying for his Tour card in 1971 and failed Qualifying School for a record 16 times before finally making it in 1982—on his 17th try. (From 1975 through 1981, the school was held twice a year.) It was truly a classic case of perseverance for a man who supported himself as a cook, dishwasher, busboy, caddie, and funeral home worker while trying, year after year, to become a Tour pro. He won over $1 million by 1990.

Did you know that Gary Player can sing? In 1970, Player recorded an album entitled *Gary Player Sings*. On the disk are renditions of "Deep in the Heart of Texas" and "When the Saints Go Marching In."

Jesper Parnevik learned the game by hitting floating golf balls into the lake behind his home in Sweden. Adding to his reputation as a Swedish meatball, Parnevik first turned up the bill of his cap to catch a tan and wound up shooting a terrific round. Now he won't play unless the bill of his hat is pointing up.

John Henry (J. H.) Taylor was one of the members of the Great Triumvirate of Golf in the early days of the sport. Harry Vardon and James Braid were the other two. Taylor, who won the British Open five times and was runner-up on four other occasions, was a dour, shy man. Once, when his fellow club members wanted to give him a party to celebrate one of his championships, Taylor deliberately took the train to a stop past the golf club so he would not have to go to the party.

Although Bobby Jones was one of the greatest golfers of all time (he won the U.S. Open four times), he never won any money in golf. Despite being a world-class player and competing against all the best pro golfers of his time, Jones remained an amateur throughout his career and never accepted money for winning a golf tournament.

Ben Hogan always believed the first hole was the most important one. One time, he and Claude Harmon were playing at the Seminole Golf Club in Florida, tuning up for a Masters tournament. After Ben birdied the first hole, he explained to Claude why that was so important: "If you don't birdie the first hole, how can you birdie them all?"

Calvin Peete, golf's Horatio Alger, fell from a tree as a young boy and broke his left elbow. He was never able to straighten his arm and had the additional setback of having to teach himself how to play golf, starting at age 23. Despite these handicaps, Peete won 12 tournaments on the PGA Tour.

Nick Faldo emerged as a dominant player in golf in the 1990s, but he wouldn't have been so successful on the links if his mother had her way. Mrs. Faldo wanted young Nick to become a fashion model because, she said, he had "smashing legs."

Nick Faldo is somewhat of a late bloomer when it comes to golf. He didn't start playing the game until he was 14 when he saw Jack Nicklaus on TV and decided to take up the game. It was a wise decision. By 2001, his Tour earnings had topped $4.5 million and he had won three British Opens and three Masters titles.

At the height of his career in 1930, the great Bobby Jones said he didn't find success on the golf course until he all but eliminated the careless stroke. Explained Jones: "The little thing that has done most to win five championships in four years . . . is simply to save that one little stroke a round that used to get away from me through carelessness or dumb play."

The great amateur champion Bobby Jones had no trouble drinking—he was something of a legendary tippler—but his stomach got so keyed up during tournaments that he often was unable to eat anything at all. It wasn't unusual for Jones to put away plenty of corn whiskey, and then fast during competition because he couldn't keep anything down. He would lose from seven to 10 pounds over the course of a four-day tournament.

The Beau Brummels on today's PGA Tour have nothing on that old clotheshorse Doug Sanders. At the peak of his preening years, Sanders's closet held more than 200 pairs of slacks and over 100 pairs of matching, multihued shoes. Sanders once explained that the clothes kept him slim because if he gained an inch on his waist, "I'd have to send out 200 pairs of slacks for alterations."

Astonishing but True Golf Facts

At the 1963 World Cup at St. Nom la Breteche near Paris,
Christy O'Connor of the Irish team was so badly hung over
that he asked a sportswriter to haul a pot of black coffee into
the woods adjacent to the first fairway and wait there.
O'Connor then hit his tee shot into the woods, walked in and
gulped the black coffee. Full of caffeine, O'Connor went on to
shoot a three-under-par 69 for the round.

Walter Hagen was extremely confident and seldom fretted
between rounds. At four A.M. the night before the final round
of the 1929 British Open, Hagen was playing cards. Someone
mentioned that Leo Diegel, who was leading Hagen by two
shots, had been in bed for hours. "He may be in bed, but he
won't be asleep," Hagen said. Diegel three-putted eight holes
the next day, finishing third, seven strokes behind the
winner—Walter Hagen.

Intriguing Facts About Famous Golfers

When Walter Hagen was about to play in the PGA
championship at Olympia Fields near Chicago in 1925, he
walked into the locker room before the tournament and
confronted Al Watrous and Leo Diegel. In a loud voice, the
superconfident Walter asked, "Well, who's going to be second?"
Walter then beat the two golfers in match play and won the
championship.

When Walter Hagen won the British Open at Royal St.
George's in Sandwich, England, in 1922, the first-prize money
was £100. Walter gave the entire amount to his caddie.

In his early professional golf career at the age of 20, Walter
Hagen not only gave golf lessons to members of the Country

Club of Rochester, New York, he also taught tennis, ice skating, and croquet.

Gene Sarazen's double eagle in the 1935 Masters is one of golf's most amazing shots, but there's a little-known story behind it. The night before, a friend gave Sarazen a "lucky" ring that he said had belonged to Benito Juarez, a 19th-century Mexican statesman. Just before Sarazen hit his famous eagle, he took the ring out of his pocket and rubbed it for luck. His friend later confessed that he made up the story about the ring. The truth was he had bought it from a street vendor.

Sam Snead once roomed with Ben Hogan during a tournament. Snead was awakened in the middle of the night by the grinding of Hogan's teeth. The next day Snead mentioned Hogan's teeth-grinding to fellow competitor Jimmy Demaret, who said, "Don't worry about it. That's just Ben sharpening his blades for today's round."

When Jimmy Demaret accepted the Masters trophy at the presentation ceremony in 1950, he told the crowd that he could best express his thoughts by singing a popular song. So he proceeded to render a chorus of "How Lucky You Are."

Elizabeth Hanley, well-known Irish champion golfer of the 1930s, was on her deathbed at the age of nearly 90. She called her favorite nephew to her bedside and whispered these final words to him: "Never give anybody more than three strokes a side."

In his illustrious career, there was at least one shot that Ben Hogan knew he couldn't make. It happened at the 1951 U.S. Open at Oakland Hills Country Club in Birmingham, Michigan. His second shot at the uphill 8th hole went over the green and up a steep slope. Hogan pitched the ball down and watched it run 25 feet beyond the cup. He lamented to playing partner Jimmy Demaret, "It was impossible." Demaret then turned to the gallery and announced, "Ladies and gentlemen, when Ben Hogan says a shot is impossible, it is impossible!" Despite the bogey 5 on the hole, Hogan still managed to win the tournament.

Walter Hagen was well known for his gamesmanship. In a special 72-hole match in 1920 against Abe Mitchell, Hagen was four down after 36 holes. Hagen then kept Mitchell waiting on the first tee for 30 minutes before the start of the second half of the match. Mitchell was so upset over the long wait that Hagen beat him 2 and 1 for the $3,000 prize.

Golfing legend Sam Snead learned to play barefoot while growing up in the mountains of Virginia. So it only seemed natural for him to play a practice round shoeless before the 1942 Masters—much to the shock of the prim and proper officials at Augusta National.

Cary Middlecoff had the unfortunate habit of waggling his club from behind the ball, up over it, and then back again. Confronted with a 240-yard second shot to the 17th hole at Meadowbrook in the 1947 Motor City Open, Cary waggled his club an amazing 22 times before finally swinging his club. The ball ended up on the green and Cary birdied the hole.

Astonishing but True Golf Facts

LPGA pro Pat Hurst trembled at the hard-earned victory at the Nabisco Dinah Shore at Mission Hills Country Club in Palm Springs in 1998. It wasn't that she was overcome by her heady victory. It was that she couldn't swim. Tradition there dictates winners take a dip with tournament officials at the lake by the 18th green. Hurst went in up to her knees, then quickly backed out.

Vijay Singh, the 1998 PGA champion, is the only world-class golfer to come from the island of Fiji and is the only Tour player ever to hold a club professional position in Borneo. He learned the game from his father, an airplane technician and golf instructor. The name Vijay means "victory" in Hindi.

Intriguing Facts About Famous Golfers

In 1956, Clifford Roberts, chairman of the Masters Committee, received a letter describing a promising young player who had just won the South African Open. The letter told of the golfer's abilities and regional conquests and said, "We would hope that he might be invited to the Masters, in which case we would pass the hat to pay his expenses." Roberts cabled back, "Start passing the hat, invitation in the mail." Thus, Gary Player was introduced to the U.S. golfing public.

Harry Cooper, a great golfer who came close but never won the U.S. Open, was very superstitious. He felt that green was an unlucky color for him. One day, his wife appeared on the course wearing a green dress. He waved her off the course and wouldn't let her return until she had changed her dress.

Astonishing but True Golf Facts

The Wilson Sporting Goods Company sent Masters Champion Gene Sarazen to the 1954 U.S. Amateur championship at the Country Club in Detroit to check out a young golfer. "He lunged at the ball and he duck-hooked everything," Sarazen recalled. "He had to hole long putts and get up and down out of the sand to win the title. I told Wilson the kid would never amount to much. The kid was Arnold Palmer."

In his early days, Walter Hagen signed autographs for his fans as "W. C. Hagen." Then he went to England and found out that "W. C." meant the water closet, or bathroom. From then on, he signed autographs as "Walter Hagen."

Unusual Facts About
Tournaments and Courses

At midnight, September 25, 1928, four of the better golfers at
St. Andrews played a two-hole match, the 1st and the 18th, by
the light of fireworks, car headlights, and Chinese lanterns. Of
the nearly 500 spectators who were on hand, six fell into the
famous Swilken Burn because they didn't see the ditch in the
dark of the night. The match was declared halved.

As late as 1974, the Old Course at St. Andrews, Scotland, was
played in reverse order. For example, golfers on the 1st tee hit
to the 17th green. Next, they went to the 18th tee and drove
their balls to the 16th green, then they hit from the 17th tee to
the 15th green, and so on. Golfers played in reverse order every

other year to give the fairways a rest. By playing this way, the Old Course could recover from many of the scars of the previous year, since the majority of the divots would be in different areas on the course.

Florida club pro Mike Bender won the 1998 North Florida PGA Match Play Championship without really trying—because his scheduled opponent, Ron Philo Jr., couldn't get the day off to play the final match. Ironically, Philo, of Amelia Island, Florida, operated a golf school.

Anybody who thinks sand greens are a silly way to sharpen your game for big league competition should consider some of the past champions who've competed and won sand greens titles as youths. Past winners include 1996 U.S. Open champion Steve Jones, three-time Open champion Hale Irwin, and PGA touring brothers Tom and Curt Byrum.

The plucky Brits didn't let anything as tiresome as the Battle of Britain keep them off the links. They simply modified the rules. At St. Mellons Golf and Country Club, players were asked to collect bomb and shell splinters from the fairways to prevent damage to mowers. Players also noted carefully, at risk of great personal harm, the red flags marking the position of delayed-action bombs in the rough.

In the 1920s, on the old Welwyn Garden City Golf Course in New York, players often carried cutting shears in their golf bags. That's because the fairways had especially tall grass. The course rules allowed a player to use the shears if the tall grass interfered with his shot.

Astonishing but True Golf Facts

The mysterious Count d'Alcardi may have paid the most ever for a single hole of golf. The count, an eccentric who made the rounds in the 1910s on the French Riviera, paid more than $650,000 to have his own course built near his country estate—and then quit the game in a huff after making a 15 on the 5th hole. The course was soon plowed under.

The most interminable women's match in tournament history was won by Mrs. Edwin Labaugh of Paterson, New Jersey, who took the city championship in the early 1900s after 88 extra holes were played.

It took a sudden death that was far from sudden to bring to an end the longest playoff in Senior Tour history and give Bob Murphy the 1997 Toshiba Senior Classic title. Murphy and Jay

Sigel went nine extra holes before Murphy sank a stunning 80-foot putt to win. Since only the 16th, 17th, and 18th had been designated as playoff holes, Murphy and Sigel circled the circuit a full three times. "I was getting dizzy," Sigel said. "We went round and round and round."

Samuel Ryder is named after Samuel Ryder, a businessman from Lancashire, England, who made his fortune selling packets of seeds for a penny. Ryder (1858–1936), who loved golf, first proposed a biannual match between English and American golfers in 1926. The following year, in the first Ryder Cup match, the Americans prevailed 9½ to 2½. When Ryder died nine years later, he was buried with his favorite five-iron.

Astonishing but True Golf Facts

Bobby Jones's triumphs are well documented, but the gentleman golfer suffered one stunning upset that got surprisingly little press. In 1926, in a winner-take-all challenge match with Walter Hagen, Jones was defeated 11 and 10 at St. Petersburg. Hagen won $8,500, a record amount for the time, and he then presented Jones with a set of shirt studs and cuff links.

Flooded fairways forced officials to cancel the 1996 AT&T Pebble Beach National Pro-Am. The washout marked the first time in 47 years that a PGA Tour event was called off on account of rain.

The never-ending U.S. Open playoff in 1931 at the Inverness Golf Club in Toledo, Ohio, is likely never to be repeated. In it, George Von Elm and Billy Burke, who wound up in a tie for the title with 72-hole scores of 292, both shot 149 in the subsequent 36-hole playoff. Von Elm, the more consistent player, shot another 149 in the second 36-hole playoff. But Burke shot 148, or they might still be playing.

Small matters like weddings cannot be permitted to interfere with the club championship. That was the message of Captain Gerald Moxom who, on his wedding day in 1934 in England, hurried from the chapel in Bournemouth to his club in West Hill, Surrey. Still dressed in his tux, he shot a round of 71 in just 65 minutes to win the competition.

One of the more unusual matches in golf history was between Harry Vardon and his partner, who were using golf clubs, and F. M. A. Webster and his partner, who were using javelins.

Distances in the 1913 event were adjusted and the javelin throwers had only to hit within a two-foot square to "hole out." The golfers easily prevailed, 5 and 4. Webster's longest drive, er, throw, was 160 feet.

Have your club call my club: The first known instance of a golf match by telephone occurred in 1957 when the Cotswald Hills Golf Club in Cheltenham, England, won a match against the Cheltenham Golf Club in Melbourne, Australia, by six strokes. The match was open to every member of both clubs, and the aggregate score was phoned in to England. Cotswald won 564 to 570.

The Olympic Club is such a brutal layout that many famous writers have slashed it with their poison pens. The sprawling, mangled cypress trees were described by writer O. B. Keller as looking like "they had been designed by a man who had gotten drunk on gin and tried to sober up on absinthe." Jim Murray of the *Los Angeles Times* called the Lake Course "the John Wilkes Booth of golf courses" and "a Bolshevik of a golf course."

You don't want to build a golf course on land whose ownership is disputed by Indonesian farmers. After feeling they'd been unfairly compensated by the owners of a golf course, irate farmers in 1998 carved in huge letters down the middle of a plush fairway, WE ARE TAKING WHAT IS OURS. Golfers were given a free drop if their balls landed on the letters.

At Para, Brazil, the golf course owner supplied golfers with black disinfectant soap that they used to lather their whole bodies. When the lather dried, the golfers looked as if they had just emerged from a coal mine. But they didn't mind. The dried lather warded off nasty black flies that harassed unprotected players.

In 1998, England's Skipton Golf Course had been targeted by a serial bomber who had detonated a series of explosions along the course's 14th fairway. The manager of the club, Gary Potter, tried to look at the bright side of the bombings: "Well, at least it has cured the mole problem."

The 27 holes at spectacular Banff Springs Golf Club in Canada's Banff National Park are among some of the most beautiful on the planet. The course is in immaculate condition, except for inch-deep spike marks. Rude golfers?

Nope. The spike marks are really from hooves of the herd of 1,000-pound elk that roam the course at will. Because it's a national park, the elk have free rein and, pity the greenskeeper, they have unhindered access to every fairway, bunker, and green.

The banana-peel-on-the-staircase award goes to the grounds crew at Valderrama Golf Course in Spain for their work at the 1997 Ryder Cup. Believing the Jim Furyk–Lee Janzen vs. Colin Montgomerie–Bernhard Langer match would never reach the 18th hole, the crew mowed the green. But when the match reached the final hole with the U.S. team down 1, Janzen, unaware of the maintenance, rocketed his 50-foot birdie putt 15 feet past the hole.

The Tournament Players Championship course at Sawgrass Stadium in Florida was quickly transformed from friendly to fierce after the 1994 TPC—when Greg Norman cake-walked to a 264, averaging an impressive 66 per round. Red-faced Tour officials, who had been promoting the Players as "golf's fifth major," made sure the toothless old course grew some fangs by creating new, rock-hard greens. Lee Janzen's winning score in 1995 was a 283, the biggest one-year swing for a tournament played on the same layout in PGA Tour history.

You want to play Riverside this weekend? Get in line. The National Golf Foundation says that 46 courses are named Riverside, including six in Texas alone. Rounding out the top five names for courses are Lakeview, 40; Rolling Hills, 38; Hillcrest, 37; and Lakeside, also 37.

Par for the United States, it seems, is 114,737 strokes. At least that's what it took Floyd Satterlee Rood to play the country when he went from coast to coast from September 14, 1963, through October 3, 1964. He lost 3,511 balls on the 3,397.7-mile course that went from the surf of the Pacific to the surf of the Atlantic.

Astonishing but True Golf Facts

Mike "Radar" Reid surprised lots of his golfing colleagues before the first round of the 1998 U.S. Open when he said he loved the rough at the Olympic Club, adding he wished they played a course like that "every two months." His frustrations rose in concert with his scores and by Sunday, after he had finished at 16-over 296, he had changed his tune. "If we played courses like this regularly," Reid said, "the only decision would be razor blades or gas."

Through 2001, the following states have hosted the most major championships: Georgia, 67; New York, 24; Pennsylvania, 23; Illinois, 19; Ohio, 18; California, 13; Michigan, 11; Massachusetts, 10; New Jersey, 9; Minnesota, 7; and Oklahoma, 7.

The Greater Greensboro Chrysler Classic decided to commemorate the 60th anniversary of Sam Snead's first victory at the long-time Tour stop by unveiling a trophy dedicated to the man who won eight Greensboro titles between 1938 and 1965. The Sam Snead Cup is now presented to victors of the tournament. Ironically, despite all his wins there, Snead never received a single plate, cup, or trophy for his efforts.

The first televised broadcast of a golf tournament was at the 1947 U.S. Open at the St. Louis Country Club in Clayton, Missouri. However, it was beamed to a local audience only. The USGA did not see fit to go nationwide with the broadcast of a tourney until seven years later, when TV viewers across the country were treated to the 1954 U.S. Open. The following year, the Masters was televised for the first time.

Astonishing but True Golf Facts

When South Carolina golf resorts took out **rain insurance** policies for their guests, many golfers thought it was funny when the word *snow* was added to their policies. But it was no joke when Myrtle Beach was hit with two inches of snow in January 1992. Forty-eight golfers at the Sands Oceanfront collected $7,100 from the resort for lost playing time.

Talk about dedication. One man prepares for the British Open by not eating or drinking a single thing 24 hours in advance of the tournament. No, it's not an eccentric golfer. The man is Ivor Robson, the tournament's first-tee starter. He says he wants to ensure he can remain vigilant at his post for eight hours without heeding nature's call.

Unusual Facts About Tournaments and Courses

The silver Claret Jug presented to the champion of the British Open is not kept by the winner. It must be returned to the Royal and Ancient Golf Club, which displays the jug in its trophy case. Starting in 1880, the winner was given an inexpensive medal made of gold, silver gilt, and a base metal as a keepsake award. When Willie Park won the medal in 1889, he sent it back to the club, feeling that if the cheap award was the best the R&A could do, the club would be better off keeping it. The jug eventually replaced the medal, but the tradition of leaving the award at the R&A remains.

Before each Masters tournament, the previous year's winner gets to select the menu for the champion's dinner. Among the choices selected by past Masters champions: Nick Faldo, 1996, fish and chips; Ben Crenshaw, 1995, Texas barbecue; Jose Maria Olazabal, 1994, bluefish and garlic, oil, and perejil sauce;

Bernhard Langer, 1993, turkey and stuffing, German wedding soup; Fred Couples, 1992, chicken cacciatore.

After 21-year-old Tiger Woods won the 1997 Masters at Augusta, he selected his menu for the champion's meal: cheeseburgers, grilled chicken sandwiches, french fries, and vanilla and strawberry milkshakes. It was the first time anyone at Augusta ever ate french fries because club cofounder Clifford Roberts had deemed them unhealthy and forbade their presence on the club's regular menu.

Jerry Pate won the 1982 Tournament Players Championship at the TPC at Sawgrass. To celebrate the victory, Pate threw PGA Tour commissioner Deane Beman and course architect Pete Dye into a greenside pond and then jumped in himself.

Unusual Facts About Tournaments and Courses

In 1949, Dr. Cary Middlecoff and Lloyd Mangrum tied for the championship of the Motor City Open at Meadowbrook Country Club in Detroit. They played 11 playoff holes without a decision until darkness finally brought an end to the marathon. So the officials called the tournament a tie, with both players splitting first- and second-place prize money worth $2,500 each. Although the split was sanctioned, it was common for pros to secretly agree to split first- and second-place money before a playoff began.

The famous Old Course at St. Andrews is a public golf course owned by the City of St. Andrews, Scotland, which graciously permits play by various clubs, such as the Royal & Ancient Golf Society. In 1876, the Championship Committee of the R&A failed to make arrangements in advance for the British Open, so the competitors had to share the course with the townspeople on a first come, first served basis.

Astonishing but True Golf Facts

The first U.S. Open Championship, played at the Newport Golf Club in Rhode Island in 1895, was almost an afterthought. It was an added event following the first U.S. Amateur Championship. Only 11 players—10 Englishmen and a Canadian—played four nine-hole rounds in a single day in front of fewer than 200 spectators. The winner of the first Open was Horace Rawlins, an English pro who scored 45-46-41-41–173, and received $335 and a $50 gold medal for his victory.

Here's an interesting oddity about the Old Course at St. Andrews, Scotland: The par ratings of the individual holes form an 18-hole palindrome. They read the same way backward and forward: 444-454-434-434-454-444.

Pebble Beach hosted its first national tournament in 1929, when it was the site of the U.S. Amateur Championship. In the final match, Jimmy Johnston played his third shot to the 18th hole from the beach. He had to wade out into the surf and wait until a wave had receded far enough to allow him to stroke his ball. Johnston went on to save par and eventually won the event 4 and 3 over Dr. O. F. Willing.

The oldest golf course bridge is nearly 1,000 years old. The stone bridge over the Swilken Burn at St. Andrews dates back to about A.D. 1000. There was no golf course there at that time . . . mainly because golf had yet to be invented.

The 1913 U.S. Open championship at the Country Club in Brookline, Massachusetts, was postponed from its original date in June until September in order to allow Harry Vardon and Edward Ray to complete an exhibition tour before playing in the tournament. Francis Ouimet won the Open in a historic playoff with Vardon and Ray. Ouimet shot 72 to Vardon's 77 and Ray's 78.

The Curtis Cup, the Women's International Cup trophy, is named for two sisters—Harriet and Margaret Curtis. Harriet was the USGA women's champion in 1906 and Margaret was champion in 1907, 1911, and 1912. The magnificent silver trophy is engraved: "To stimulate friendly rivalry among the women golfers of many lands."

The Royal and Ancient Golf Club is royal, but not as ancient as the Honourable Company of Edinburgh Golfers, which formed in 1744, 10 years before the institution of the R&A. One group, however, claims to be older. The Royal Burgess Golfing Society says it was founded in 1735.

Unusual Facts About Tournaments and Courses

William Garner was a golf fanatic who lived to play the game. He always said that when he died he wanted to spend eternity on the links. He passed away in 1967 at age 75. So, according to his wishes, his friends took his ashes to the Croham Hurst Golf Club. There, his fellow club members granted his wish, but with one little prank of their own. They scattered his ashes over an area of the 17th hole where he spent most of his time—130 yards out and in the rough.

One of the longest singles match playoffs ever occurred when William Barksdale Jr. defeated John Scurry on the 33rd hole—18 holes at match and then 15 more in overtime. It happened in the second flight of the club championship at Forest Lake Country Club in Columbia, South Carolina, in 1985.

Bizarre Bets

A pair of hard-nosed gamblers gladly took hustler Titanic Thompson's bet that he could hit a golf ball an unbelievable 500 yards. The only stipulation was that the ball had to be driven from a tee, but it didn't have to land on a fairway. In the dead of winter, Thompson hit his shot onto an iced-over lake. The ball was still rolling as Thompson pocketed his money.

In 1966, 55-year-old English amateur golfer Harold Dean won a strange £20 bet. He played the Dukenfield course in Manchester, England, swam one mile, and drank three pints of beer—all within two hours.

Bizarre Bets

David Strath bet all comers in 1876 that he could negotiate the bunkers and huge greens of the Old Course at St. Andrews in fewer than 100 strokes . . . in the dark. With only the full moon and a full complement of bettors to accompany him, Strath shot 95, and didn't lose a golf ball. In his memory, the front bunker on the 11th hole at St. Andrews was named the Strath Bunker.

American Willie Hunter won the British Amateur Championship in Hoylake, England, in 1921 after spending almost all his money to get there. He bet his last $10 at odds of 33 to 1 on himself to win. After finishing first, Hunter won $330—a windfall for a penniless golfer.

During a 1936 four-ball match, Richard Scott and Joe "Clown Prince" Ezar were 4 down to Michael Scott and Bobby Locke with five holes to play. Joe asked Richard if he had ever seen five birdies in a row. Richard said no. Ezar bet $500 that he could do it, then, amazingly, bagged five consecutive birdies to win the match one up.

You've heard of playing at night, but playing *as* a knight? That was the case for singer Harry Dearth who, on a bet, played a challenge match back in 1912—clad in a complete suit of armor. Dearth, playing at Bushey Hall, England, clanked to a 2 and 1 defeat.

Gambling golfers know that the term *Nassau* has nothing to do with the island in the Bahamas. But most don't know that the first Nassau match was played in 1900 at the Nassau Country Club in Glen Cove, New York. There is no record of when the first "press" was applied.

Pro Ky Laffoon teamed up with notorious golf hustler Titanic Thompson to create one of the greatest golf cons in the game. Thompson would roll into a town and challenge golfers to a game. With Laffoon as his shabbily dressed caddie, Titanic would win and then turn to his opponents and declare, "Hell, my caddie can beat you guys." He would then offer the hustled players a chance to win their money back at double or nothing by beating his caddie. The suckers took the bait and flopped as the incognito pro whipped them.

Astonishing but True Golf Facts

Stanley Turner went off as a 6–4 underdog one day in 1921 when he tried to play a five-mile distance from his house in Maclesfield, England, to the Cat and Fiddle Inn, in fewer than 170 strokes. Mr. Turner made out quite well in negotiating the difficult terrain, shooting 64.

Payne Stewart had the pants beat off him after making a wacky wager during the 1988 Leukemia Classic exhibition match in Wilmington, Delaware. Playing against a trio of top women golfers, Stewart bet he'd beat their best score per hole—with the loser doffing their pants. The women rose to the challenge by defeating Stewart, who lived up to the agreement and removed his famous knickers, causing a squeal from the shocked gallery.

Bizarre Bets

Many golfers carry their golf bags, but in full battle gear? That's what Nick Farrar did on a wager just before World War I broke out. The wager was 10 to 1 that Farrar couldn't go around England's Royston Links in less than 100 strokes wearing his full infantry gear, water bottle, field kit, and haversack. He shot a 94.

The Honorable Guy Butler, a 12 handicapper, played the Kingswood course in Surrey, England, in 1973 with a croquet mallet. It took him 151 shots, including only 33 putts. Butler easily won a bet that he would finish the round in fewer than 250 strokes.

Leo Diegel used to hustle 15 handicappers back in the 1930s by offering to play the front nine off his right foot, and the back nine off his left. When he had a pigeon far enough down, he'd play him double or nothing with his feet crossed. And he'd win that bet too.

🟡

Wagers are deeply woven into the fabric of golf. And fabric is what L. T. Wainright needed at Scotland's Monifieth Links across the firth from St. Andrews. There, on a winter day in 1923, Wainright played 18 holes *au naturel* because earlier that spring he lost a bet that he would shoot lower than 80 before the winter came. Unfortunately, he lost more than his shirt.

🟡

In the 1940s, one of the favorite scams of hustler Titanic Thompson was betting he could make three out of five putts from 30 feet away. He usually won by sinking four. What his victim didn't know was that Thompson would go out on the course the night before and place a heavy water hose from the cup to the edge of the green. This created a nearly imperceptible trough that the tricky Thompson would use to send putts easily into the hole.

After Tiger Woods won the 1997 Masters, a British bookmaker offered 50 to 1 odds that the golfer would be elected president of the United States by the time he turns 50. One gambler wagered £200.

In 1907, John Ball Jr., one of England's greatest amateur golfers, accepted a bet that he could play Hoylake in dense fog in under two hours, 15 minutes—and not lose a ball. The golfer played with a black ball, shot an 81, and beat the time limit too.

Astonishing but True Golf Facts

Before the 1930 season began, pro Bobby Cruickshank made a
bet that the great Bobby Jones would win all four major
tournaments (the U.S. Open and Amateur and the British
Open and Amateur championships) that year. The odds of that
happening were 120 to 1. Jones wound up winning all four
majors and Cruickshank enriched himself by $60,000.

During the winter of 1898, Freddie Tait, a famous amateur
golfer from St. Andrews, bet that he could play from the
clubhouse at Royal St. George's in England to the clubhouse at
Royal Cinque Ports Golf Club—a distance of about three
miles—in 40 teed shots. Tait did it easily—hitting his thirty-
second shot through a window at the Cinque Ports club.

Bizarre Bets

Harry Vardon, who won the British Open championship six times from 1898 to 1914, was the pro at Ganton Golf Club in North Yorkshire, England. He was so good that he got bored with regularly beating the club's members. Vardon began playing left-handed, from scratch, and gave the members their full handicap allowances. But it didn't matter. Vardon still won with monotonous regularity.

During an ESPN interview, John Daly, a self-confessed compulsive gambler, admitted that he bet on the European team to win the 1995 Ryder Cup at Oak Hill. Daly, the reigning British Open champion at the time, said he made the bet because he was angry at being left off the U.S. team. Daly didn't reveal how much he won.

Darren Clarke didn't let losing a $33 private bet to Colin Montgomerie shake his confidence. The bet was made during a practice round at the 1998 Benson and Hedges Open in England. But when it really counted, Clarke, a native of Northern Ireland, won the tournament by shooting a final-round 67 for a 273 total. His take, minus the bet to Montgomerie, who finished tied for fifth, was $206,967.

Interesting Facts About Golf Gear

The unofficial record for playing the most rounds with the same golf ball belongs to Judge Michael Nehemiah Manning of Talladega, Alabama. He bought a Pro-Flite ball on November 15, 1928, and retired it on January 28, 1929, after completing 46 rounds of 18 holes each. His average score was 82, about 2,000 blows, not counting putts.

In 1934, Horton Smith—the Missouri-born pro known as "The Joplin Ghost"—captured the inaugural Masters tournament by a single stroke over Craig Wood. Horton won with the help of a Bobby Jones model driver that he had borrowed from fellow competitor Paul Runyan.

Astonishing but True Golf Facts

Advertisements for steel-shafted golf clubs appeared in the magazine *American Golfer* as early as 1914. The Bristol Company brought out a set of rectangular shafts that had oblong holes cut in all four sides to reduce wind resistance. The result was that they hummed and whistled when they were swung. After 18 holes, the golfer felt as if he had been playing a harmonica. The clubs were not a success.

Dick Jackson has done as much to popularize the game of golf as have Tiger Woods and Arnold Palmer combined. The Houston auto dealer loved the game, but arthritis was preventing him from enjoying it. So he took his expertise and his money and invented the "Arthritis Special"—golf's first gas-powered cart in 1948.

Interesting Facts About Golf Gear

Johnny Miller was the first Tour player to use a 47-inch-long putter in competition at the 1982 L.A. Open. He tried it in the hope it would cure him from the dreaded yips. Unfortunately, it didn't. He swears he's used every conceivable brand of putter to cure the yips and still hasn't found the perfect solution.

When Harry Vardon, six-time British Open champion, won the 1896 Open, he carried only seven clubs. At the height of his career, Tom Morris Sr., four-time British Open champion, toted only five clubs—one wood and four irons.

In 1930 Bobby Jones won the "Grand Slam of Golf"—the Amateur and Open championships of both the United States and Britain—using hickory-shafted clubs. Although steel shafts had been allowed in Britain for a year, Jones had not yet convinced himself that they were better than the old hickory ones.

For fear of commercializing his pure golfing moment, astronaut Alan Shepard never revealed what type of balls he struck on the moon. But Jack Harden, his pro at Houston's River Oaks Country Club, knew. They were range balls. Harden's son, Jack Harden Jr., said his father knew the balls would be subjected to extreme temperatures and wanted something durable. The balls were two-piece Surlyn-covered Spaldings with blue stripes and PROPERTY OF JACK HARDEN emblazoned on them.

When Sam Parks Jr. won the U.S. Open at Oakmont in 1935, he went against convention and carried two putters in his bag. Instead of adding an extra wood or iron to his legal limit of 14 clubs like the other pros did, Parks kept a Spalding Cash-In for long putting and the other for holing out.

Young Tom Morris—who won the British Open championship in 1868, 1869, 1870, and 1872—retired as champion. But he was best remembered for unwittingly destroying his clubs. He would waggle his club so furiously that sometimes the shaft would break.

Wayne Levi was the first tour player to win a tournament with a disco-era, orange golf ball. He did so at the 1982 Hawaiian Open. In 1996 Levi was presented with a memento of the event at the 14th anniversary of the feat when tournament officials gave him an orange ball.

Astonishing but True Golf Facts

Since its invention more than 50 years ago, the golf cart has opened up the game to couch potatoes who feel they're still getting some exercise playing golf. There are more than 750,000 golf carts, or "golf cars" as the manufacturers prefer to call them, operating in the United States today.

There was no golfer quite like funnyman Jackie Gleason. His golf set consisted of 12 woods with mink club covers and only two irons—a wedge and a putter. He played with gloves on both hands. Jackie was also known to drive his golf cart right through the middle of sand bunkers.

Obviously, white balls are the choice of golfers. Orange balls comprise less than 1 percent of Wilson's total golf ball sales, despite arguments from physicists that orange is the most visible color in the rainbow. The only place golfers are apt to see an orange ball is at a driving range or mini-putt park. Interestingly, yellow balls outsell orange ones.

Gibby Gilbert was disqualified from the 1973 Atlanta Classic for not having enough balls. "I started with six," he recalled. "I loaned three to my partner, Gary Player. By the time I got to the final hole, I was down to one." Gilbert immediately drove that ball into the rough. A panicked search uncovered a dozen golf balls, but none was Gilbert's brand. Realizing he had no chance to make the cut, Gilbert simply gave up and walked off the course. His partner commemorated the crazy moment by marking their scorecard ROB—for "ran out of balls."

Astonishing but True Golf Facts

Housing was at a premium during the 1957 Bing Crosby tournament, so golfers Porky Oliver and Eddie Darrell were forced to room together. The next day at the 3rd tee, Oliver complained to his roomie that his feet were killing him. Darrell responded that his shoes seemed loose. After an awkward moment, the men realized they were wearing each other's shoes and traded on the spot.

In rushing to make his flight from Florida to the 1967 Hope Invitational in California, Tom Nieporte mistakenly packed a mismatched pair of golf shoes. Both shoes were black, but one was plain while the other sported a wingtip. Nieporte made it through the tournament—which he wound up winning—without a single comment about his fashion faux pas from fans, colleagues, or officials. But, as he stood proudly on the victory stand, Nieporte noticed an official staring intently at his shoes. After the ceremony, he approached the sharp-eyed official and remarked, "I have another pair just like this in Boca Raton."

How much did Greg Norman love his King Cobra oversized Ti prototype driver? Enough that when his regular driver broke at the 1996 Doral-Ryder Open, the Shark had his wife hop in a

After PGA pro Brandel Chamblee discovered his luggage had been stolen upon his arrival at the Houston Airport in 1998, he borrowed clothes from his fellow golfers—including a pair of Willie Wood's underwear—before the Shell Houston Open Pro-Am. "I made everything I looked at," said Chamblee, giving undue credit to the briefs. "Next week I think I'll wear Ben Crenshaw's underwear. Imagine how I'll putt then."

How much did Greg Norman love his King Cobra oversized Ti prototype driver? Enough that when his regular driver broke at the 1996 Doral-Ryder Open, the Shark had his wife hop in a plane and fly a similar model from their home in Hobe Sound, Florida, 82 miles away to the course near Miami. Norman then went on to win his second straight tournament using the trusted Ti. A month earlier, he used the club and won the Australasian Ford Open.

Have you ever lost a favorite putter or driver to the deep waters of a pond or the thick brush of the rough? The club registration and retrieval service SafeKeeper estimates that nearly 4.5 million clubs are lost annually, with a financial loss of more than $300 million. Experts figure that 75 percent of the lost clubs never make their way back to their owner. The orphaned clubs are usually chucked into the lost-and-found bin at golf clubs all across America.

Ben Hogan was one of the most precise golfers on the PGA Tour. "At the U.S. Open one year, Hogan got a shipment of new balls," recalled pro Harvie Ward. "He opened up the carton, took out a magnifying glass and looked at each ball, one by one. Every so often, he tossed a new ball into his shag bag. I couldn't believe it, brand-new balls. Finally, I asked him why. Hogan explained, 'Some of the dimples have too much paint on them.'"

Astonishing but True Golf Facts

Texas pro John Bredemus always played with old, discarded golf balls. But the penny-pinching tactic backfired during the Los Angeles Open after his opening drive landed deep in the rough. During the search for the lost ball, Bredemus's caddie came upon an old, scarred ball and threw it away. Unfortunately, it turned out to be the Texan's lost ball. As a result, Bredemus was disqualified from the tournament after only one shot.

At the 1997 MCI Classic, Woody Austin began beating himself on the side of his head with his club after his 35-foot putt at the par-3 14th hole stopped well short of the cup by a full 15 feet. Members of the gallery gasped as the golfer grasped his putter by its club head and started flailing away at himself. Austin's five head cracks were designated Shot(s) of the Day on ESPN's *Sports Center*. After the fifth and final whack,

Austin noticed the shaft of his putter had bent—and he had to finish the round using a sand wedge for putts.

The first USGA National Amateur championship was held at Newport Golf Club in Newport, Rhode Island, in 1895. There were only 32 contestants, among them Richard Peters, whose specialty was to employ a billiard cue on the greens! (The rules were not as well defined then.) Unfortunately, he lost his match by 5 and 4 to the Reverend W. S. Rainsford of St. Andrews.

The colorful names for golf clubs such as *brassie, spoon, mashie,* and *niblick* came to an end when the A. H. Spalding Company introduced the first matched and numbered set of golf clubs in 1930.

In 1906 Goodrich introduced the Pneumatic—a ball with a rubber core filled with compressed air. But the ball had a tendency to explode in the air or in the golfer's pocket. Willie Dunn Jr. was using the ball in an exhibition match at St. Andrews when it exploded in midair and injured a spectator. Goodrich, acknowledging the problem with the ball, promptly retired it. The ball was eventually outlawed.

Bobby Jones had more than one putter called "Calamity Jane." In 1923, Joe Markle found a broken-shafted, rusted putter in a cemetery behind the green of the Nassau Country Club. He repaired it and gave it to Jones, who had been putting badly. Jones used the club to defeat Bobby Cruickshank in the 1923 U.S. Open. Then Jones had a copy of the putter made and used it from 1924 through 1930. The original club is in the Augusta National trophy case.

Interesting Facts About Golf Gear

In the 1930s, Walter Hagen played with a golf set which consisted of 20 irons and four woods. The irons were in half-steps from one to nine, that is one, one and a half, two, two and a half, and so on. Of course, this was before the 14-club limit was established by the USGA. Walter's bag and equipment weighed about 40 pounds.

Golf's frustrations sometimes become too much to bear, and such was the case with John Cason. According to newspaper accounts, Cason was playing a round at LeJeune Golf Course in Miami in 1961 when he hit one tee shot too many behind a tree. Cason calmly went to his golf bag, pulled out a .38 caliber revolver, and shot his golf ball. Unfortunately for Cason, the act was witnessed from an adjacent fairway by a sheriff's deputy, who cited him for discharging a firearm.

Astonishing but True Golf Facts

At the 1955 U.S. Open championship, Jack Fleck used a new set of Ben Hogan irons. Hogan was so anxious to have Fleck use the clubs in the tourney as a promotion that he personally delivered the pitching and sand wedges to his competitor. Later, Hogan was stunned when Fleck defeated him with Ben's own clubs.

Mashie was the old term given to the five-iron, but it had nothing to do with mashing the ball. It's derived from the French word *masse*, the same term used today to describe the backspin put on a billiard ball.

In the 1950s, at the treacherous, wind-beaten, 110-yard 7th hole at Pebble Beach, Sam Snead faced strong gusts. Afraid that the wind would carry his nine-iron shot into the ocean,

Snead teed off with his putter and deliberately bounced his ball down the hill and into the front bunker to avoid the traditional shot. He parred the hole.

In 1939, Arthur Benson of Newcastle, England, established the standard for the lowest score with a weird implement—he shot a 76 at Knowles Park, a 6,547-yard course, using only a cricket bat. He even putted with it, employing a sidesaddle method like a croquet player.

Joe Kirkwood, the winner of the 1920 Australian and New Zealand Opens, was an accomplished trick-shot artist who wielded what was believed to be the world's longest club—a special driver that measured 10 feet long. Joe also swung the world's tiniest club—an 18-inch wedge.

Astonishing but True Golf Facts

During World War II, when there was a severe rubber shortage, golfers had to improvise. A wooden golf ball championship was played at Potchefstroom, South Africa. The winner was A. A. Horne of Potchefstroom, going around the course in only 90 strokes.

Alan Shepard hit the first lunar golf shots in 1961 with a six-iron that is now on display at USGA Museum in Far Hills, New Jersey. But what about the balls? Shepard speculated the 400-degree daily temperature changes on the moon must have exploded the two balls. But Eric Hayne, a spokesman for the Jet Propulsion Laboratory, felt the durable spheres are still playable. "They can be in nothing but pristine condition," said Hayne.

Interesting Facts About Golf Gear

Until 1920, the golf ball was teed up on a mound of wet sand.
But then a dentist in Maplewood, New Jersey, William Lowell,
hand-whittled some tees from a wooden flagpole in his front
yard, and created the "Reddy Tee." Although the tee was
patented in 1925, there have been many imitators because the
patent application was written too loosely.

Nick Faldo was so disgusted with his putter at the 1998 Macau
Open he elected to use a nine-iron on the greens for six holes
during the final round, actually sinking three birdie putts. When
asked what he planned to do with the putter, Faldo suggested he
might throw it out of his helicopter on the way home.

Golfers can gaze in awe at one of the most famous sand wedges
in golf history. Willie Turnesa donated his wedge to the USGA

museum in Far Hills, New Jersey. Turnesa, the 1938 and 1948 U.S. Amateur champion, used that lucky wedge to get up and down in two shots from bunkers on 13 occasions on his way to victory in 1938.

Sam Snead never mistook his ball for that of another player, because the Wilson Company imprinted special balls just for him with the number zero on them.

The world record for balancing golf balls one on top of another, without adhesive, belongs to Lang Martin of Charlotte, North Carolina. Martin stacked seven golf balls on a flat surface in 1980, according to the *Guinness Book of World Records*.

Interesting Facts About Golf Gear

Golf balls were very scarce in 1945 at the Los Angeles Open. As a result, Sam Snead played the entire tournament with one ball—and he won. "You couldn't get balls then, because of the war-time rubber shortage," he recalled. "I was paying $100 a dozen for balls. Before the tournament, Bing Crosby gave me a ball, a Spalding Dot, and I played with it throughout the four rounds. The cover was loose, but it kept going."

In 1921, amateur golfer Emmett French played the difficult Pinehurst golf course with no other club but his putter. Despite that difficulty, French scored a creditable 80 on the 18-hole course.

Astonishing but True Golf Facts

If you were to lay golf balls dimple to dimple from the first golf club at St. Andrews, Scotland, to Augusta, Georgia (site of the Masters Tournament)—a distance of about 6,100 miles—you would need 230 million golf balls.

Outlandish
Caddie Incidents

Caddie John (Cubby) Burke found himself in the line of fire when he was plunked at the 18th hole of the 1997 Canon Greater Hartford Open. The shot was launched 215 yards away by his golfer, Brad Faxon. The carefree caddie had been strolling along the left side of the fairway when—*thwack!*—Faxon's drive drilled him in the back, leaving the caddie with a big, purple welt. Yet Faxon hurt more after the miscue—because he had to take a two-stroke penalty, which led to a double bogey.

In 1997, the winnings of an LPGA Tour hole-in-one pool went to the caddie of the golfer who scored the ace. At that year's

Astonishing but True Golf Facts

U.S. Women's Open, Susie Redman nailed a hole in one in the first round to win $1,700 for her caddie—who just happened to be her husband, Bo.

Jack Nicklaus decided to caddy for his son Gary at a PGA Tour qualifier in West Palm Beach, Florida, in 1997. The Golden Bear showed up bare-legged in shorts—an infraction of the Tour's dress code for caddies. Not wanting to fail his son, Jack quickly slipped into a pair of rain pants while waiting for his wife, Barbara, to arrive with a pair of his slacks. It was all to no avail. Gary shot a 78 and failed to advance.

A wisecracking caddie who knew a thing or two about pressure helped Larry Ziegler end a championship drought. At the 1998 Saint Luke's Classic in Belton, Missouri, Ziegler had Hall of

Outlandish Caddie Incidents

Fame baseball player George Brett carrying his bag. "I tried to make him laugh at least once a hole," Brett said. "Otherwise I just tried to stay out of his way." It worked. Ziegler's victory was his first in nearly seven years—a gap between wins that's a Senior PGA Tour record.

Winning the British Open in the early days of golf was no guarantee of future wealth. Robert Ferguson—champion in 1880, 1881, and 1882—spent the latter part of his life so poor that he had to work as a caddie at Royal Musselburgh, the scene of one of his British Open victories.

In 1914, during World War I, there was a scarcity of professional caddies in Great Britain. With customary British ingenuity, country clubs experimented with dogs as bag carriers and ball finders. One player said, "I expect to see dogs universally in the future. With a dog as your caddie, there is no one to hear you swear and no one to make fun of your play." The experiment flopped because the dogs were more interested in chasing rabbits than finding golf balls.

A fielding error by his caddie cost Mark Brooks two penalty strokes at the 1992 Las Vegas Invitational. At the 18th hole, Brooks tossed his ball to his caddie for a cleaning. But the caddie missed the ball and it rolled into the water hazard alongside the green. Brooks took off his shoes and socks and went into the water to retrieve it. He found 18 balls, but none of them were his. Brooks was penalized for not finishing the hole with the ball he had played from the tee and finished well down the money list.

Joe Horgan was the dean of American caddies and admired Harry Vardon greatly. One time Horgan was caddying for a pro who landed in a trap but hit a remarkable recovery dead to the pin. The pro asked: "What do you think of that shot, Horgan? Could Vardon have got out the way I did?" Horgan noted, "Get out? Mr. Vardon would never have gotten in!"

Caddie Paul Bramlett rooted so hard for his golfer that he turned an eagle putt into a bogey at the 1978 Quad Cities Open in Coal Valley, Illinois. Leonard Thompson hit his third shot on the par-5 10th hole for what looked like an eagle. But a cheering Bramlett had accidentally dropped a tee that deflected the ball away from the cup—and cost Thompson a two-stroke penalty.

In the final round of the 1932 British Open, Gene Sarazen badly shanked a shot on an early hole. His caddie put the iron away in the golf bag and said, "We won't be requiring the use of that club anymore, will we, Mr. Sarazen?" Gene didn't touch the club the rest of the day, and won the tourney.

Kermit Zarley lost his head after the first round of the 1997 BankBoston Classic. He played most of the first round with only 13 clubs. That's because the head snapped off his three-wood when it caught on a rope under which his daughter Monica, who was caddying for him, tried to maneuver the golf cart.

A caddie's shortcut at the 1987 Tournament Players Championship cost Raymond Floyd two penalty strokes and his temper when the golfer whacked a 260-yard drive that came down smack dab into his golf bag. Floyd's soon-to-be ex-caddie had taken a shortcut to the 11th fairway from the 10th green and placed the golf bag on the edge of the rough.

At the 1996 Marks & Spencer Open, Kristel Mourge d'Algue hit a beautiful drive that landed within inches of the pin on the par-3 4th hole. Yet she walked away with a double bogey 5. Why? Because Kristel's caddie had handed her the Callaway seven-iron she had asked for—but mistakenly pulled the club from another player's bag. After incurring her two-shot penalty, d'Algue two-putted the hole—and then fired the caddie on the spot.

While playing in Scotland on the Queen's Course at Gleneagles, the wife of USGA official George Smith sent her tee shot on the 13th hole into a thick stand of heather. After she and her caddie searched for several minutes, Mrs. Smith declared the ball lost. However, the club carrier continued to search. "You can stop looking for the ball now," said Mrs. Smith. But the caddie replied, "It's not the ball I'm looking for, mum . . . It's yer clubs I've lost."

Outlandish Caddie Incidents

Rex Caldwell's caddie should have received combat pay or at least a purple heart following the 1987 AT&T Pebble Beach National Pro-Am. Back-to-back embarrassing accidents occurred on the 18th hole when Caldwell first nailed caddie "Lost Lee" Stehle in the chest with a ricochet shot off the branch of a tree. Then Caldwell accidentally smacked Stehle in the face with his wedge while slamming the club down into his golf bag.

For sheer arrogance on the golf course, Archie Compston had no peer during his playing days in the 1920s and 1930s. One caddie just wouldn't do. Compston employed three: one to tote his bag; another to carry his sweater, raincoat, and umbrella; and a third whose sole responsibility was to take care of his smoking paraphernalia.

Zany Fan Behavior

Gary Player was practicing a very difficult shot out of a bunker at the 9th hole at Oakland Hills, getting ready for the 1961 U.S. Open. He was exploding shot after shot to within a few feet of his chosen spot on the green. A spectator remarked, "Gee, are you ever lucky!" Gary replied, "Yes, and the more I practice, the luckier I get."

Corrine Dibnah of Australia won the 1988 Women's British Open Championship by a nose . . . of a spectator. On the 2nd hole of a sudden death playoff with Sally Little, Dibnah's drive was off line and struck a man on the nose. But fortunately for the golfer, the ball rebounded onto the fairway. Unfortunately for the spectator, his nose was broken. Because of the lucky break, Dibnah was able to halve the hole. She then won the tournament on the next hole.

Horton Smith, the tall, handsome Masters winner in 1934 and 1936, was once offered a cigarette by a female spectator. He refused. The girl asked, "Don't you drink, either?" Smith shook his head. "No vices, honey?" she asked. "Sure I have," replied Smith. "I'm often short on my long putts."

Mark O'Meara won the 1998 British Open with a little help from spectator Martin Holmes. Holmes, a 12 handicapper, found O'Meara's lost ball in the rough at Royal Birkdale's 6th hole, giving the contender a free drop, rather than a lost-ball penalty. Strokes from such a penalty would have cost O'Meara a shot at the playoff with Brian Watts, which O'Meara eventually won. O'Meara got the Claret Jug and $492,000 in winnings. Holmes got a ball signed by O'Meara, not to mention his gratitude.

Spectators who were trying to be helpful wound up hurting the game of Dave Marr at the 1965 Bob Hope Open. First, Marr hit an approach shot that bounced off the green and rolled 130 yards past the hole—thanks to the fans who parted from the ball's path. Then on the very next hole, where members of the gallery stood their ground, Marr's ball hit a fan and bounced into a sand trap.

In the 1933 International Four-Ball at the Miami Country Club, Paul Runyan and Horton Smith were partners. On the 4th hole, Runyan's wayward five-iron second shot struck fan

Dr. John Nelson right on the top of his head and knocked him out. The next year, in the same competition, Smith hooked his drive on the 9th hole and struck a spectator in the hip. Who was it? The same Dr. Nelson! Fortunately, he wasn't as badly hurt as he was the first time.

An overzealous fan offered a handshake to Gary Player after the final round of the 1962 Masters and squeezed Player's hand so hard that the golfer thought it was broken. It was only sprained, but Player, golfing with a bandaged hand, lost in a playoff the next day by three shots to Arnold Palmer.

Crowd favorite Macdonald Smith needed only a final round 78 to capture the 1925 British Open, but his enthusiastic fans cost him a chance for his first-ever win. Although Smith had emigrated from Scotland to the United States, thousands of rowdy Scots turned out to cheer him on. At that time there were no gallery ropes to control the crowd. The mob swarmed Smith at every hole, making it almost impossible for him to concentrate. He struggled to a second-place 82—and never got close to winning another tournament.

Walter Burkemo, winner of the 1953 PGA Championship, had his game knocked way off course during a tournament when an inquisitive fan innocently asked, "How come when you address the ball, you sometimes take four waggles and other times you take five?" Burkemo wrestled with the question and bogeyed the next three holes trying to figure out the answer.

Lloyd Mangrum had a short putt for par on the 9th hole at Red Run Golf Club in the 1948 Motor City Open. His ball just barely reached the front of the cup and then dropped in after hanging a fraction of a second. A lady spectator said, "That wasn't a very good stroke, Mr. Mangrum." Lloyd replied, "Are we playing *how* or *how many*, lady?"

When the gallery didn't show enough appreciation for his nice drive, Tommy "Thunder" Bolt quit the 1962 Philadelphia Classic—in the middle of the 12th hole. Bolt's tee shot had curved out over a water hazard and landed 10 feet from the cup. But the crowd remained mum. The irritated golfer instructed his caddie, "If that isn't good enough, go pick up my ball." Tommy then bolted off the course.

Jeff Sluman was about to attempt a five-foot putt for the win on the second playoff hole of the 1987 Tournament Players Championship when the crowd broke into cheers and laughter. The commotion was over a fan who, after making a bet, dove into the water surrounding the green. Sluman stepped back, tried to regain his composure—and proceeded to miss his putt. A hole later, he lost the tourney.

Zany Fan Behavior

In recalling the early days of golf tournaments, Sam Snead said, "Fans would come right down the fairway and follow you into the rough. One time, a bunch of kids were fighting over my divots. As soon as I'd swing, they'd grab a divot and run. They'd say, 'Next one's mine.' I learned later that they were taking the divots home and planting them in their yards for souvenirs."

Greg Norman's gracious reaction to his heartbreaking choke in the 1996 Masters, when he blew a six-shot final-round lead, earned him fans that a green jacket never could have. He said strangers stopped him on the street to say that the classy way he dealt with the loss changed their lives and gave them new perspective. Lost a tournament, changed a life. Not a bad deal, Norman thought.

Surprising Age-Related Golf Facts

In 1967, Ben Hogan shot a blistering 30 on the back nine at the Augusta National Masters course. The score equaled the nine-hole record at that time. What made the feat even more remarkable was that he did it when he was 53 years old.

Old Tom Morris Sr. was the grandfather of the British Open. Since the Open was first played in 1860, Morris competed in 36 straight tourneys. He won the first of his four Open champions at age 40 in 1861. He competed in his last Open in 1896—at the ripe old age of 76.

Surprising Age-Related Golf Facts

Ray Floyd, on turning 50 and becoming eligible for the PGA Senior Tour, said, "I went to bed on September 4, 1992, and I was old and washed up. I woke up a rookie. What could be better?" After becoming eligible for the PGA Seniors, Floyd won his first senior tournament the following Sunday. That made Floyd the first golfer in history to win on both the PGA and Senior Tour in the same year. Floyd had earlier won the PGA Tour's Doral Ryder Open in March.

Bobby Jones was only 14 years old when he won the Georgia State Amateur championship. He qualified that year, too, to play in the U.S. Amateur championship at Merion, and went to the third round before he lost in match play.

Astonishing but True Golf Facts

Teenage phenom Matt Kuchar tied for twenty-first at the 1998 Masters, becoming the second youngest to finish in the top 24 at the age of 19 years, nine months, and 23 days. But youth was certainly served in 1979 when Bobby Clampett tied for 23rd at the tender age of 18 years, 11 months and 24 days.

In 1996, Tiger Woods was no babe in the woods when he garnered his third pro win in just his ninth tournament. The achievement is noteworthy because it took golfing great Jack Nicklaus 26 events to register his third win. Phil Mickelson needed 31 tourneys, Arnold Palmer 53, Greg Norman 67, and Tom Watson a whopping 134 to collect, respectively, their third victories.

Surprising Age-Related Golf Facts

In 1996 Karrie Webb became the first non-Senior golfer to win $1 million as a rookie. Karrie's crowning achievement came at the LPGA's inaugural ITT Tour Championship in Las Vegas. The 21-year-old Australian's four-stroke victory against the other top 29 LPGA money winners earned her a $150,000 paycheck—and pushed her winnings over the magical million-dollar mark.

Jack Nicklaus was arguably golf's greatest player in the 20th century. A sampler: He shot 51 for his first nine holes at age 10. At 11, he shot 81 for 18 holes. By age 12, he routinely broke 80. At 13, he was a three handicapper and had broken 70. By age 16, he had won the Ohio Amateur. At 19, he won the first of his two U.S. amateur titles.

Astonishing but True Golf Facts

At the age of 20 years, seven months, 19 days, Se Ri Pak became the youngest woman to win an LPGA major in 30 years when she captured the 1998 McDonald's LPGA Championship. She's the fourth youngest ever to win an LPGA major. Sandra Post, at 20 years, 20 days, won the LPGA Championship in 1968. Patty Berg was only 19 when she won the 1937 Titleholders championship, and Betty Hicks was a record 17 when she notched the Western Open that same year.

Jack Nicklaus was the oldest player ever to finish in the top 10 at the Masters when he tied for sixth in 1998 at the age of 58 years, two months, and 21 days. Sam Snead was second when he tied for 10th in 1967 at 54 years, 10 months, and 12 days.

Justin Rose created a sensation in the golf world in 1998 when, at age 17, he finished two strokes behind winner Mark O'Meara at the British Open. However, John Ball Jr. was 16 when he won the Claret Jug in 1890. Still, he was a seasoned veteran compared to Tom Morris Jr., who won the Open in 1868 when he was just 14 years, four months, and four days old.

Astonishing but True Golf Facts

Grandmother Maureen Paladino, 65, was six years older than the combined age of her three nearest competitors when she won the 1998 Women's Golf Association of Western Pennsylvania title, her second championship. The first was in 1956. She'd given up the game to marry and raise a family. She admitted the 42-year break from competitive golf had made this win a toughie. "It was all I could do to keep my mind together," she said. "I'm no young chicken, you know."

Three-time champion Gary Player became the oldest player to make the cut at the Masters in 1998, but never threatened the leader board and ended up dead last among players who finished 72 holes. Still, the 62-year-old Player took pride in the fact that he outshot a notable field of contenders including past champions Nick Faldo, Nick Price, Tom Watson, and Ben Crenshaw, all of whom failed to make the cut.

Surprising Age-Related Golf Facts

Gay Brewer was 66 when he became the oldest player to shoot par 72 at the Masters in 1998 (although he later failed to make the cut). In his par round, he became one of just a handful of Augusta players who were within eight shots of shooting his age. The others were: Gene Sarazen, 74 at age 68; Arnold Palmer, 74 at age 66; Doug Ford, 81 at age 73; and Sam Snead, 74 at age 66.

Tiger Woods complied an impressive rookie streak of five consecutive top-five finishes at the end of 1996. The previous player to do that was Curtis Strange in 1982—in his sixth year as a pro.

Golfers can play a lifetime without ever getting an ace. Geoffrey Stephenson was in preschool when he scored his first hole in one. In 1997, the four-year-old Marco Island, Florida, boy aced the 5th hole at Ironwood Country Club using a scaled-down driver from the ladies' tee, 65 yards out. According to the *Guinness Book of World Records*, he's the youngest ever to score an ace.

Three septuagenarians defied the odds in 1990 when each of them aced the 159-yard 3rd hole at the Ponte Vedra Inn & Club near Jacksonville, Florida—within a 90-minute span. Ridge Wilson, 70, Eugene Sanford, 72, and John Vyverberg, 77, all used five-irons.

Odd Animal Encounters

In 1985, Dave Hickler was playing the par-3 17th hole at the Bangkok Country Club in Thailand when he hit his tee shot into a water hazard. Amazingly, the ball bounced out of the water and onto the bank. In an incredible stroke of luck, the ball had struck a foot-long carp that was swimming near the surface of the water!

LPGA pro Sherri Steinhauer was literally outfoxed when she was playing the 6th hole in the 1990 McDonald's Championship at the DuPont Country Club in Wilmington, Delaware. After she drove her ball in the rough, a fox ran out of the woods, grabbed the ball, and buried it in a bunker on the next hole. Steinhauer was allowed to drop another ball in the rough and replace the original ball with a new one because the fox had chewed it. The golfer was assessed no penalty because the fox was considered an outside agency.

In 1921 Peter McGregor got an assist from an insect on the final hole at Scarborough South Cliff Course in Yorkshire, England, to win his match. McGregor and his opponent, Harry Dowie, were at the last hole dead even. McGregor needed to sink a long putt to win. His putt stopped right on the edge of the cup. But then a grasshopper leaped on the ball and knocked it into the hole.

Over a 10-year span from 1980 to 1990, Waddy the beagle found an astounding 39,954 lost golf balls on the Brockenhurst Manor Golf Club in Brockenhurst, England. Whenever someone lost a ball on the course, Waddy, who was owned by club secretary Robert Inglis, was dispatched to the rough to locate the ball.

The wise men who set forth the Rules of Golf were thoughtful enough to consider a rule to cover ball-snatching seagulls. In 1998, during the second round at the Players Championship, a seagull picked Brad Fabel's ball off the island green and dropped it into the nearby water. Fabel was allowed to place a new ball where the old one had first come to rest. But he bogeyed the hole anyway.

In 1985, Art May was a little short of the 200-yard 7th hole at Pruneridge Golf Club in San Jose, California. His ball had stopped on the fringe near a small gopher hole. Just as May was about to chip, a gopher popped out of the hole, slapped the ball with its tail, and then disappeared back into the hole. The ball rolled onto the green, where May proceeded to drain the putt.

Kevin Burress's tee shot at the 130-yard 16th hole at Arroyo Del Oso Golf Club in Albuquerque, New Mexico, landed near a duck's nest. The duck waddled over and nudged the ball into her nest next to five eggs. Then she settled down to defend them. Burress managed to retrieve his ball by using his club to distract the duck.

Bill Graves was playing at the Dania Golf Club in Florida in 1985 when a land crab crawled out of its hole, grabbed his ball, and took it back with him underground. Green was unable to recover his stolen ball, so he was allowed a free drop with another ball.

Playing in the 1960 U.S. Open at Cherry Hills, Tommy Bolt hit consecutive drives into the lake at the 18th hole. When a carp jumped out of the water as he teed up another ball, Bolt became so enraged that he fired his driver at the fish and killed it. But by doing so, Bolt also drowned his driver.

Astonishing but True Golf Facts

All it took was one X ray for doctors to find out what was ailing Hannah, a three-year-old yellow Labrador retriever from Cherry Hill, New Jersey. In 1997, the tail-wagging companion of owner Scott Sullivan spent her evening hours retrieving balls for Scott while he worked on his short game. Only one problem—her enthusiasm got the better of her. Doctors removed nine balls from her aching belly.

"Worm weather" forced a bizarre delay during the third round of the 1997 Scandinavian Masters. Attracted by the sight of a sea of wriggling worms on the freshly cut 5th fairway, a flock of hungry crows clogged the course and delayed the tournament for 25 minutes. Officials finally were able to shoo the birds by having a groundskeeper mount a mower and make mulch of their squirmy smorgasbord.

Odd Animal Encounters

In 1956, George Wiehl, a golfer in St. Joseph, Missouri, stepped up to the tee and whacked a long drive down the fairway. He watched with satisfaction until it came to a sudden halt. A woodpecker, flying the other way, had impaled the ball on its beak!

In 1985, W. E. Jackson was playing on a Jacksonville, Florida, course, when a 200-pound wild boar charged him and a companion. Jackson defended himself with a five-iron, killed the boar, and literally "brought home the bacon."

In 1928, two members of England's Burton-on-Trent Golf Club were engaged in a singles match when one of them was fleeced by a lamb. After Arthur Wheeden landed his approach shot on the green, a lamb picked up the ball and deposited it in the hole. Wheeden had to replace the ball to its original spot. Wheeden proved he didn't need the lamb's help after all, because he holed his putt to close out a 4 and 3 victory.

In the Senior/Junior Tournament of 1981 at the El Dorado Hills Golf Club in California, David Heagy, a junior player, hit a shot into a slanted underground drainage pipe barely larger than the ball. Recalled Heagy, "There was no way to retrieve it, but as we watched in disbelief, the ball slowly rose up and out of the pipe. Directly behind the ball, and pushing it, was a toad."

Other Extraordinary Golf Facts

Going into the final match of the 1969 Ryder Cup at Royal Birkdale, the United States was tied with the Britain/Ireland team. Jack Nicklaus and Tony Jacklin were all even on the last hole after each player hit the green in two shots. Jacklin rolled his eagle putt to within three feet of the pin, while the Golden Bear overshot his by five feet. Nicklaus made his birdie attempt and then picked up Jacklin's coin, conceding the match to a tie, even though Jacklin might have missed the three-foot putt. It is considered one of the most gracious acts of sportsmanship in history.

Astonishing but True Golf Facts

Today's superstars like Tiger Woods and Greg Norman may not blink while signing multimillion-dollar endorsement deals, but golf was a much different game for the touring pros 50 years ago. Legendary Byron Nelson earned a grand total of $182,000 for his entire career and in 1945 put together an amazing streak of 11 consecutive tournament wins. The phenomenal feat did earn him one memorable perk. "Wheaties . . . I got a case of Wheaties and $200," Nelson noted in 1997. "But not until I'd won seven or eight tournaments in a row."

An attempt to shame a "tortoise" into speeding up his play failed miserably at the 1922 Scottish Amateur Championship. Some of the frustrated golfers brought a full-sized bed to the course and lounged upon it while the deplorably slow player, identified only as R. Wells, slowly sized up his shots. The couch potatoes got plenty of rest—because for the remainder of the tourney the slowpoke puttered about even longer between shots.

Other Extraordinary Golf Facts

A man who falsely identified himself as New Mexico golf pro Bo Britt played three holes during the 1988 British Open practice round before his cover was blown. The bogus Britt shot over 10 on each of the first two holes and had just launched his 11th shot at the third when officials politely asked him to leave.

In 1997, bored bean counters employed by Jack Nicklaus at his golfing business Golden Bear estimated the long-playing legend had logged 170,061 strokes during the 2,405 rounds he'd played as a professional. They also tallied the distance Jack had covered while playing golf over that same time frame. Nicklaus's journey to golfing greatness had taken him a leg-numbing 9,620 miles—a total more than three times the distance from New York to San Francisco.

Four Scottish golfers were so dedicated to their sport that even the death of their longtime playing partner couldn't stop their weekly routine. In 1996, Jimmy Hogg, 77, collapsed and died from a heart attack just moments after teeing off at the first hole of a regularly scheduled round of golf in Fife, Scotland. Jimmy's four friends watched somberly as the ambulance took their friend away—and then they played on. Said one member of the foursome, "I'm sure Jimmy would have wanted us to do that . . . he would have done the same."

When Fred McLeod defeated Willie Smith in a playoff for the 1908 U.S. Open championship, Fred weighed only 108 pounds—the lightest golfer ever to win the tourney.

The National Association of Short Adults says that playing golf makes you shorter. There is scientific proof that a player shrinks .01 inches during an 18-hole round, because the player's spine is constantly compressed when he is upright for several hours straight. That means that after 7,200 rounds, a six-foot golfer would completely disappear!

The Turnesa family was one of the most amazing in golf history. All seven brothers became famous golfers. Six of them—Mike, Frank, Joe, Phil, Doug, and Jim—played on the PGA Tour. The seventh brother, Willie, didn't want to be a pro. But he became a world-class amateur, and won the U.S. Amateur Championship in 1938 and the British Amateur Championship in 1947.

Caryl Meeks, of Stamford, Connecticut, buried some of the ashes of Stephen Signore, her longtime companion and an avid golfer, on the 9th fairway of Sterling Farms Golf Club—the public course where he played until his death in 1997. No one would have been the wiser, except that the ashes were dug up by the course superintendent's dog.

On the lunar surface, the amount of energy expended on a 300-yard drive would, if it were possible to swing so freely in a spacesuit, send a golf ball a distance of more than a mile. That's because the moon has one-sixth the gravity of earth.

Tom Jewell is a self-admitted golf fanatic—and a very polite one at that. Since 1987, he has, without fail, written letters of congratulation to every winner of every single PGA, Senior PGA, and LPGA tournament.

Making the cut and advancing into the next round of a 1968 tournament saved Ken Venturi from a fiery death. Venturi had booked a seat on a flight out of Houston just in case he failed to make the cut. The pro put together a round good enough to keep him grounded for at least one more day. Hours later, the plane for which Venturi held a ticket tragically crashed, killing all on board.

Astonishing but True Golf Facts

A National Demographics and Lifestyles study said there are seven things golfers do less than the average U.S. citizen: read the Bible; sew; work on their cars; do knitting and needlework; eat health foods; read science fiction; and own a cat.

An average round of golf in the tropical splendor of Hawaii will run you $85.70, the highest of any average in-season weekend green fee with cart, according to the National Golf Foundation. Rounding out the top five of pricey rounds are: Nevada, $84; Arizona, $66.70; California, $57; and Colorado, $51.90.

Improving one's golf game is good for business. A study by *The New York Times* of 51 CEOs found that the lower their handicaps, the better their companies' stocks performed. Tell that to the boss the next time he busts you for working on your short game during company time.

In an era before huge purses, it took golfing legend Arnold Palmer, the fourth all-time tournament winner with 60, 13 years to earn $1 million. In 1996, Tom Lehman won two tournaments, had 13 top-10 finishes, and earned $1,780,159, slightly less than Palmer's career earnings figure of $1,904,673.

Lee Elder, Jim Dent, and Chuck Thorpe quietly posted a first when the trio played together in the final round of the 1998 Bell Atlantic Classic. Tour officials said it was probably the first time an entire threesome in an official PGA Tour or Senior PGA Tour event was comprised of African-American golfers.

Astonishing but True Golf Facts

In the 1988 U.S. Women's Open, play was moving so slowly that pro Lori Garbacz decided she would make a statement. On the 14th hole of the first round, she had her caddie go up to a nearby pay phone and order a pizza that she wanted delivered to the 17th tee. Sure enough, the pizza was waiting for Garbacz when she reached that hole. She had plenty of time to eat the pizza, too, because there were two groups ahead of her waiting to tee off.

The first American woman to win an Olympic gold medal was Margaret Abbot, who shot a 47 in the ladies' nine-hole final at the 1900 Games in Paris. Abbott, who hailed from Chicago, told relatives that she won the tournament "because the French girls apparently misunderstood the nature of the game and turned up to play in high heels and tight skirts."

Other Extraordinary Golf Facts

In the 1933 British Open, which was played at St. Andrews, Scotland, Denny Shute defeated Craig Wood for the title. When he won, Shute became the first champion to shoot the same score, 73, for each of his four rounds.

When Charlie Sifford competed in the 1961 Greater Greensboro Open at Sedgefield Country Club, it was the first time that a black golfer was permitted to play in a PGA-sponsored event in the South. Sifford played well enough to finish fourth.

The tallest man ever to win a PGA Tour event is lanky Phil Blackmar, who captured the 1997 Shell Houston Open in a big way. The towering victor stood an impressive six feet, seven inches in his socks—a full inch taller than former pro George Archer. Blackmar beat Kevin Sutherland on the first hole of sudden death to win $288,000—more money than he had made in any of his previous 13 seasons.

How did the term *bogey* become part of golf lingo? In the early 1900s, a British golfer played a hole in one over par. Referring to the "Colonel Bogey March," which was popular at the time, the golfer told his playing partner, "Even Colonel Bogey could have done better than that!" From that time on, a score of one-over was called a bogey.

The expression "O.B.," which stands for "out of bounds," is believed to have been coined in Ireland in the 1930s at Ballybunion. There was a graveyard to the right of the 1st hole and Finbar O'Brien's farm beyond it. Many a tee shot was either "in the graveyard" or "O.B."

Other Extraordinary Golf Facts

During Prohibition, at least one official report called golf "as dangerous as bootleg gin." In the report, written in 1922, the federal director of Prohibition enforcement for Minnesota gave these four reasons why golf was bad for family men: "First, golf is not intended for anybody under 55 years of age. Second, it encourages idleness and shiftlessness. Third, men neglect their families and their business duties to play the game. And, fourth, young men are tempted to take on expenses they cannot meet and so frequently are led to commit crimes."

In a 1772 book entitled *Sermons to Gentlemen About Temperance and Exercise*, there is this simple reference to golf—the first known printed remark in America about the sport: "Man would live 10 years longer of using this exercise once or twice a week." The book was written by Dr. Benjamin Bush, a

Philadelphian who had studied medicine at the University of Edinburgh in Scotland.

The use of the word *birdie* originated in 1899 at the Atlantic City Country Club when George Crump, who later designed Pine Valley Golf Club, was playing the 350-yard 2nd hole with Ab and William Smith. Ab's second shot stopped six inches from the pin. "That was a bird of a shot," Ab cried. One-under on a hole has been called a birdie ever since.

The earliest mention of golf in Scotland—the birthplace of the sport—was a pronouncement by the Scottish Parliament in 1457. It decreed that golf "be utterly cryit doune and not usit" (rejected and ignored) because it was keeping young soldiers away from archery practice.

Other Extraordinary Golf Facts

Did the Italians invent golf? The oldest known activity resembling golf was a Roman game called paganica, played in an open field with a bent stick and a leather ball stuffed with wool. The theory is that the Romans brought the game with them when Julius Caesar led the invasion of Britain in 55 B.C.